Teaching child development

Teaching child development

Cynthia Reynolds

B T Batsford Limited
London and Sydney

First published 1975
ISBN 0 7134 2990 9

Printed by Tinling (1973)
Prescot, Lancs
for the publishers
B T Batsford Limited
4 Fitzhardinge Street
London W1H OAH and
23 Cross Street, PO Box 586
Brookvale, NSW 2100
Australia

Contents

Preface   7

1 Why courses in child development are necessary   9

2 Organisation of courses   18
What kind of course and for whom?   18
How much time?   20
Which teachers will be involved?   21
What contribution can be made by people who work outside the school?   22

3 Aims and objectives of courses   25
Parental role and emotional needs of children   28
Importance of communication and language development   30
Child's need for play   32
Nutrition and physical care   33

4 A unit scheme and learning resources available   36
People who contribute to a learning situation   37
Resources available for use in a learning situation   37
   Adolescence   41
   Family and kinship   44
   Marriage   46
   Conception and birth   48
   Growth and development of a baby   50
   Growth and development of a young child   53
   Children in special circumstances   59

5 Learning experiences relevant to the course particularly with young children   61
Family Health Centres, hospitals   61
Toy shops, Mothercare shops, museums   62
Local area and homes   63
Practical creative sessions in school   63

Playgroups, nursery classes, day nurseries, mothers' clubs　64
Preparations to be made by teachers　65
　　Playgroups; Day nurseries; Nursery classes and nursery schools;
　　Nursery centres; Mothers' and toddlers' clubs; Miscellaneous;
　　Points to note on preliminaries
*Preparation for practical experience with under fives to be
undertaken by teacher and pupils*　69
　　During practical experience; Play; Language

6 Evaluation and the future　75

Resources　85

Index　93

Preface

In January 1971 I was appointed as one of two advisory teachers, working to the Home Economics Inspectorate of ILEA, whose task was to plan courses for senior pupils in the care and development of young children. By September 1971 the first pilot courses were launched and during the following year we learned a great deal through trial and error. We are still doing so. However, by September 1972 we had gained enough knowledge to get the first two year courses under way and there has been a steady growth in the number of schools starting courses ever since. What is interesting is that there is now an enormous demand from the pupils themselves and where the courses are being offered as options, by the second year, the number wanting to take the course far exceeds the possible provision.

Repeatedly teachers say that this course involves them in more work than any other course they know of and repeatedly they come to the in-service training stating firmly that their own knowledge must be widened. Those who have now been involved for 2 or 3 years say, also, that they can't meet the demand from the youngsters for wider provision until more teachers have been given some extra training in order to cope, for this work cannot be entered upon lightly.

One of the really exciting and rewarding aspects of this work is involvement with so many people outside secondary schools who work with children in one way or another. I find that as I go round playgroups, nursery classes, etc, and meet with people who work in the community generally there is a tremendous enthusiasm for these courses. Their eyes light up and they say 'Marvellous — what a good thing' when the aims are explained to them.

Equally it is an area of study which lends itself to inter-disciplinary effort and again it is very rewarding to find a team from several disciplines creating a splendid course in a school, using one another's skills and those of people from outside the school in the best possible way.

I wrote the text of this book before the publication of the DHSS report *The Family in Society, Preparation for Parenthood* and Dr Kellmer Pringle's book *The needs of Children*. Both stress the need to prepare young people for parenthood and will undoubtedly lead to an even greater interest in courses of this kind in schools — and colleges of further education. I would like to emphasise the importance of careful preparation and slow, steady growth in courses covering Child Development and Preparation for Parenthood.

I was asked if I would write this book and put down all the information we had gathered together in these last years on the running of such courses. I have tried to do this but equally I have tried to support the thinking behind our courses by quoting the views of those who are renowned experts in their own field. I have done this quite deliberately because I think it matters that what we are trying to do is based on firm foundations. Equally, I hope this will lead to people reading more for themselves and thus acquiring a deeper knowledge of human relationships and child development prior to becoming involved in a course.

So far as the information on running courses is concerned I have tried to offer practical suggestions based on the way we have worked things out. But it should be remembered there are many different approaches and what I have written will be merely a starter.

I have read all the books and seen all the teaching packs I have suggested but I haven't seen all the films. However, those I haven't seen have been recommended by others who have used them. The unit scheme is based upon the much modified hard core scheme we have used in ILEA but as the objectives are mine and untested as yet, I accept full responsibility for their practibility or otherwise as the case may be.

I am very grateful to Miss M Walshe, Mrs P Searle, Miss A Hobsbaum and Mrs J Hawkins for reading the text and offering me constructive comments. Also, to Mrs L Scott who suggested additional resources for units where there is a link with Health Education.

I would like to express my appreciation of the work of my colleague, Mrs H Mason. We have shared the task of developing these courses and have worked both jointly and independently according to the demands of the situation. The fact is, that we have had many discussions together leading to the development of a number of ideas which have been tried out and which are now put forward in this book.

Mrs P Searle has directed my work and provided me with the necessary stimulus and inspiration to enable me to go forward as the courses have developed and grown, and I would like to thank her for all her help.

And finally, I want to dedicate this book to those wonderful, hard working and enthusiastic London teachers who have pioneered these courses; and, not to be forgotten, their young people, for without them there could never have been a book.

C R London 1975

1 Why courses in child development are necessary

Ask any teacher what his aims in education are and he will probably say to provide his pupils with enough skills to get them a job, to enable them to be responsible adults and citizens able to cope with the complexities of our society, to be good parents and people who are capable of making sensible choices, tolerant and caring for others. Existing curriculum covers many of these aims but it is only in the last few years that there has been growing recognition of the fact that there should be courses for older pupils of both sexes which are concerned with how children develop and offer some preparation for future role as parents.

As long ago as 1963 the report *Half Our Future* suggested that courses involving the study of young children could be usefully designed for mixed groups and said that partnership in marriage, whether in household chores or bringing up the children is an important concept for our society.[1]

In 1966 Winifred Hargreaves said that both boys and girls should learn about child development and a child's emotional growth, and given the opportunity, they do so with enthusiasm. She commented further that in their training all teachers follow courses in psychology and child development but not many pass on this knowledge to older pupils.[2]

At the time, both these suggestions were concerned with widening the concept of Home Economics. Because of its very nature this field of studies has always been deeply involved not only in the home but in family living and family relationships and in most secondary schools today goes far beyond the practical skills, which must never be underestimated, but are a part of the whole.

The report *From Birth to Seven* had this to say about the home and its importance for young children. 'In early life a great deal of children's development is determined by their learning at home. This is not to overlook the importance of heredity, particularly in relation to physical growth and also for intellectual development; nor to deny the influence of the wider neighbourhood and of the community. In the young child, however, the home and family play a major part in drawing out and structuring his abilities, moulding his personality and behaviour, giving direction to his interests and shaping his attitudes.[3]

This view is supported by John and Elizabeth Newson.

'The family is the fundamental social group to which humans give allegiance. Cultures vary as to how far they extend family ties and how rigidly such ties operate but the family remains the basic unit.

'Throughout the world it is normal for the process of socialisation to be initiated by the parents; it is from their behaviour towards him that the child first learns to label his own actions 'good' or 'bad'. The network of social relationships through which the process continues is gradually extended, earlier or later in the child's life according to the family and community structure of the individual culture.'[4]

It is obvious then, that the kind of family, the circumstances in which it lives and the way in which it transmits its attitudes to the child are going to affect him from birth. Scrawled on a wall in a particularly down at heel and litter laden residential street in London is this comment 'Use your birth certificate as a credit card'. How pungently the unknown writer suggests that the birthright of people affects their future in terms of 'credit' rating for life.

Child rearing is a highly complex affair and numerous factors are involved in it. The Newsons set out to study child upbringing amongst 700 families in Nottingham and were concerned to investigate all its aspects and see which influences were of particular significance. They found that class affiliated attitudes entered into almost every area of parent-infant behaviour.[5]

Not only are there differences between social classes but between races, between town and country and between geographical areas. The mother's age, the size of the family, the sex, age and position in the family of the child will also make a difference. According to Mary Farmer the personality structure of the mother appears to be of central importance. 'A mother chooses certain training methods and provides a certain social environment partly because of her own personality, itself in part the product of her own early experiences in her family of origin.'[6]

Furthermore, economic circumstances are going to make a considerable difference to any woman and the way she handles her children. If the family lives in poor housing on a low income then her difficulties will be that much greater with the likelihood of her time and temper being short so far as the children are concerned.

The Newsons say that the degree of conflict between a mother's ideals of behaviour and her environment will vary from situation to situation and from one woman to another. 'She may never be fully aware of the extent to which her treatment of the child is conditional upon her own social and material circumstances: thus the owner of an automatic washing machine may pride herself on her ability to take toilet training 'relaxedly', without pausing to probe what would be her reactions to a perpetually damp toddler if she were reduced to a sink with cold running water only . . . . Parents do not have unlimited scope for manoeuvre in deciding how they will and how they will not behave. Most parents have some basic philosophy of child rearing and most hold certain principles and values which they consider important and which they hope to implant in their children; but it is also clear that their handling of practical day to day issues is often tempered by expediency and by the necessity of coping somehow with an environment or situation not chosen by themselves.'[7]

There are, then, all these variables affecting the way in which children are brought up. Some will work favourably for the child enabling him to grow up in a climate conducive to the development of an integrated personality which enables him to take life's opportunities as they come and make reasonable or, better still, good use of them. Others will work against him and by the time he starts school at 5 years old he may be under-achieving and will continue to do so until he leaves. Not only may his job prospects be poor with an inability to stick at anything for long but instability and emotional immaturity may well affect personal relationships. Thus as a parent he may repeat the same patterns of early childhood and so we have the well worn phrases 'problem families' and 'cycle of deprivation' which are only too familiar to teachers.

There is much evidence to support the view that children from the families of unskilled manual workers are likely to do less well in school. The report *From Birth to Seven* found that at 7 years of age the chances of such a child (social class V) being a poor reader are six times greater than those of a professional workers child (social class I). Similarly the chances of a social class V child being a non-reader were fifteen times greater than a social class I child.[8]

But what takes place in school is only part of the process of education. Michael Stanton says that a good home, where parents interact with children and provide a variety of experiences usually results in early satisfactory language development. 'In this and other ways the child is equipped to take full advantage of his school education. Where there is little or unsatisfactory interaction with the child, particularly where this is coupled with overcrowding, poor child care, poor housing and other negative features, there is a strong tendency for language and concept development to be retarded.'[9]

In discussing the whole question of social class differences and attainment the authors of *From Birth to Seven* consider that heredity as well as environmental influence shape a child's ability and capacity for learning. Fully aware of the controversy surrounding heredity they nevertheless say 'that heredity plays some part in perhaps setting limits to the rate of intellectual development or to its ultimate peak can hardly be doubted. Since, in general, parents in a competitive society who have risen to occupations demanding a high level of skill will show a higher level of general intelligence than those in less skilled occupations it would follow that there will be corresponding differences in their children.'[10]

They point out that much — if not the major part — of learning takes place outside school and that much of this is accomplished within the first five years. They consider that 'a home conducive to learning is one where there is a feeling for the spoken and written word as a tool for conveying precise meaning; and where children are stimulated to question the world around them and receive explanations appropriate to their age.'[11]

They say this kind of home is not a monopoly of professional or other non-manual workers but it is found more frequently amongst occupational groups which possess a high level of education and skill. This is undoubtedly connected with child rearing patterns where the parents regard it as part of their job to educate and encourage their children and do not see it as a job to be left to teachers and schools. A study on *Success and failure in the Secondary School* by Olive Banks and Douglas Finlayson found that the majority of successful boys appeared to have close and affectionate relationships with their parents who used predominantly love-oriented techniques of discipline. Of considerable importance was the finding that parent/child relationships and techniques of discipline were more important in differentiating between the parents of successful and unsuccessful boys within the working class, than factors of a socio-economic nature.[12]

There is no reason to believe that the parents of children who do less well care any less for them than the parents of the successful child. Banks and Finlayson found that the majority of parents of unsuccessful boys were deeply and emotionally involved in their son's lack of progress, but used smacking, threats and material deprivation to try to get their sons to do better.

From Birth to Seven found that children from unskilled working class families were least often taken to 'toddler' clinics, child guidance clinics or dental clinics. That at seven years old they were relatively poorly adjusted at school with poor dental health and showed signs of delayed development in such things as bladder control, speech and physical co-ordination. Yet there was no evidence to suggest that parents in these groups had less concern for their children's welfare. Possibly the services were not seen as being relevant to the children's needs or there were simply too many problems, physical and psychological to overcome, in attending the clinics.

Probably both these reasons are valid. Being a parent is a highly skilled job and, on the whole, people have been given little chance of preparing for this demanding and complicated task. Parenthood may be thrust upon people before they are, in fact, ready for it. A study by a Professor of Child Development in the USA in 1973, of teenage parents, showed that they not only expected too much too soon from their infant children but they also slapped, shook and abused them for failing to realise their unrealistic expectations. The study found most of them were quite unprepared for their role as parents.[13]

The Newsons found that working class mothers were more likely than middle class mothers to have conceived a child before the age of 21, and that this could involve a change of role for which the mother is frequently not adequately prepared.[14]

Crellin, Kellmer Pringle and West say that commonsense would suggest that very young parents, themselves not yet fully mature emotionally, are less able to provide the emotional support and intellectual stimulation so vital to a child's optimal development. Also, being at the beginning of their working life, financial and housing problems are likely to be additional difficulties.[15]

Eva Frommer, a psychiatrist, says that 'to be a mother or father to a small baby is the deepest challenge for a human being. It is a task without visible reward, a giving without any tangible return, an interruption of a well planned life without rhyme or reason to it, a merciless unremitting emotional demand. Unfortunately parents are usually quite unprepared for this aspect of parenthood and find it a very threatening experience. It is necessary that less sentiment and more realism should enter into teaching on this subject so that new parents do not feel inadequate and guilty about their way of grappling with an entirely unexpected situation.'[16] She goes on to say that this sense of guilt and inadequacy undermines the self-respect and confidence of parents in themselves and robs them of authority with their children leading to an apparent uncaring attitude which has really grown out of resignation under an intolerable burden of parenthood for which no one had prepared them.

So, preparation for parental role including some understanding of children's needs and how to meet them is something which would be helpful and worth while for many people. But, when shall this take place? At school or later?

Michael Stanton argues that 'it would be desirable to educate for positive approaches in child rearing while mothers-to-be are still at school. This would be the first stage. Unless there is some modification of outlook and attitude before the first child arrives the young mother is more than likely to adopt child-rearing procedures familiar to her in her own environment. . .

The second stage at which this education can take place is when young mothers visit maternity clinics for pre-natal attention and during the period from birth to nursery school age when mothers are visited by health visitors. At this stage, discussion relating to child rearing practices will be much more meaningful than at school level. Being more aware of what a young child can do or respond to may result, for example, in a modification of views on punitiveness.'[17]

Certainly the idea of educating future parents while still at school is sensible for this will be the one and only time when they can all be reached — however unsuccessfully. But the idea of a second stage in this programme, for young parents, is a good one. It will reinforce work carried out earlier and as Michael Stanton says be more meaningful once the first baby is expected and later is going through the early developmental stages.

It is to be hoped that the appropriate Health Authorities, Adult Education Institutes and other bodies such as the TV services would expand the beginnings which have already been made in this direction. Often the programmes have not been geared to the needs of the less articulate, less confident working-class parents. Once involved they become extremely interested and as self-help movements like the Playgroup Movement have found, are willing to change their attitudes.

Brenda Crowe referring to the courses run for playgroup leaders (and these cut across all classes) says that once the mothers like and trust a tutor and discover that much of her experience has also been theirs they are prepared to let go many of their misconceptions and to re-learn.[18]

In a description of a mothers' club in a Liverpool overspill town, Kirkby, attached to an infants school and set up as a project to teach about children's needs one mother said 'Well, I shout now instead of beating but I'm trying hard to shout in a soft voice.'[19]

Certainly if parents are willing to change their attitudes towards their children there is every reason to suppose that young people in their mid-adolescence will be receptive towards positive teaching on the development of children, particularly when this is related to themselves and their relationships with other people. But these courses must be for both boys and girls and for all abilities.

The Newsons found that 79% of fathers took a practical part in the care of their small babies. In fact they found that 'at a time when he has more money in his pocket and more leisure in which to spend it than ever before, the head of the household sits at his own fireside, a baby on his knee and a feeding bottle in his hand: the modern father's place is the home.'[20]

It stands to reason, therefore, that boys as well as girls must learn about their children's needs. In the past when extended family networks lived in the same neighbourhood young mothers could turn to their own mothers and other relatives for help, support and advice. No doubt this still holds good for families who have not been split up by new housing projects, overspill towns and better jobs in new towns. Nevertheless today the young mother is more likely to rely on her husband for help, support and advice and with the changing roles of the present time there is no doubt that he frequently enjoys being involved in his home and family.

It is often assumed that the very intelligent can apply their intelligence to anything they have to, with successful results. This may be true for some but the fact is that bringing up children can present just as many problems in a different way. Unaware fully of a child's emotional needs a professional class family may employ a succession of *au pair* girls, thus exposing their children to frequent changes of substitute mothers from a different culture with different child rearing practices and speaking a different language.

The Newsons point out that highly educated parents often enter parenthood with the idea that coping with children is merely a matter of applying an intellectual understanding of child development to specific practical situations. 'This can lead to a rather painful and guilt-provoking confrontation with reality, when the professional class mother having committed herself heavily to the theory that friendly verbal explanations will produce rational co-operation in a toddler, finds that he is rationally unco-operative and that in practice her careful explanation tends to degenerate into an exasperated and undemocratic screech of GET ON and DO IT!'[21]

Furthermore, problems stemming from isolation and loneliness in rural areas, high rise flats and brand new semi-detached houses in the midst of new estates cut through all classes. Single parents are particularly vulnerable, and if they come from another culture and are living in an environment they feel to be hostile then their problems are even greater. Unhappiness — whatever the cause, it may be due to a breaking or broken marital relationship — will reflect on the children and the way they are handled.

So, in courses about child development and parental role it becomes essential to look at the way people interact, why they behave as they do in various situations and what circumstances may have brought about certain reactions. No one can produce all the answers but if our young people at least learn to pause and think before they rush into headlong action it should be of some help. And if they fail to always pause and think, as happens to us all, then perhaps they will reflect afterwards on what they might have done and try to do differently the next time. McPhail, Ungoed-Thomas and Chapman say that 'if you use education in learning to care you can help to build the considerate society in school and outside — a society in which people actually take each others needs, interests and feelings into consideration when acting . . .'[22]

So then, as suggested by Dr Kellmer Pringle, 'all schools should run a course in human relations and child development with particular emphasis on what is now known about the importance of the earliest years of life for optimal physical, emotional and social growth. Some first hand experience of very young children should form an integral part of such a course.'[23]

The following chapters offer some suggestions on how these courses can be organised.

REFERENCES

1   *Half our Future,* Report of The Central Advisory Council for Education, HMSO 1963
2   Hargreaves, W S *Education for Family Living* Blackwell 1966
3   Davie, Ronald, *et al From Birth to Seven* Longman 1972
4   Newson, John and Elizabeth *Four Years Old in an Urban Community*, Pelican 1970
5   Newson, John and Elizabeth *Four Years Old in an Urban Community* Pelican 1970
6   Farmer, Mary *The Family*, Longman 1970
7   Newson, John and Elizabeth *Four Years Old in an Urban Community*, Pelican 1970
8   Davie, Ronald, *et al From Birth to Seven,* Longman 1972
9   Stanton Michael 'Education for Motherhood', *Trends in Education*, October 1969
10 & 11   *From Birth to Seven* (see 8)
12   Banks, Olive and Finlayson, Douglas *Success and Failure in the Secondary School*, Methuen 1973
13   De Lissovoy, Vladimir *Times Educational Supplement*, 21.9.73
14   Newson, John and Elizabeth, *Patterns of Infant Care*, Pelican 1965
15   Crellin E, *et al Illegitimate* NFER 1971
16   Frommer, Eva *A Voyage through childhood into an adult world*, Pergamon 1969
17   Stanton, Michael *Education for Motherhood*, Trends in Education, October 1969
18   Crowe, Brenda *The Playgroup Movement*, Allen and Unwin 1973

19 Loffill, Alma 'Learning to be a better mum', *Times Educational Supplement,* 4.1.74
20 Newson, John and Elizabeth *Patterns of Infant Care,* Pelican 1965
21 Newson, John and Elizabeth *Four Years Old in an Urban*
22 McPhail, Peter, *et al Moral Education in the Secondary School,* Longman 1972
23 Pringle Kellmer, Mia *The Pre-School Comprehensives* 'Where' June 1973

2 Organisation of courses

Having then, established that these courses should form part of the secondary school curriculum for older pupils what moves are needed to get them under way?

For a variety of reasons one teacher will become enthusiastic and if by talking to colleagues others are found who are equally keen or, at any rate, interested, this will strengthen the situation right from the outset. Next, the head-teacher must be consulted. Much will depend on his reaction and it may be that he will see a course of this kind as being essential for all the fifth year and will want to plan on a much bigger scale as a result. Equally it may be that he will be ready to agree to an option within the fourth and fifth year curriculum or the six year which will generally be amongst those who stay for one year only. If the school is about to undergo or is engaged in some form of major curriculum change then the time won't be right for the innovation of a Child Development course in its own right and, in any case, the head may not be convinced that it will be a good thing.

Sometimes the inspiration for such a course comes from the head originally but whichever way it is, the fact is that there should be at least two or three enthusiastic teachers ready to work together on it.

If it is agreed in principle that such a course should run then the staff concerned will have to spend time talking together in order to make the following decisions.

What kind of course and for whom?

There is a good deal to be said for running a one year pilot course involving a smaller number of pupils, as a trial run. A good many teething problems will emerge, can be resolved and a bigger programme will run more smoothly in the second year. A comment frequently heard from teachers working in the second year of the course is 'I feel

I'm better organised this year and it's not so difficult as last year.' The fact is that the first year isn't easy but this should not discourage anyone from trying. If a pilot course of this kind takes place it is usually for sixth formers and frequently continues to exist alongside an option started up for fourth years going into the fifth year.

Is the course going to be for all the fifth years? Boys as well as girls? Academics as well as leavers? Should there be an examination? If so, what? How will the course fit into other activities such as Environmental Studies or Community Education? What about Health Education — does the school have a good scheme and should this be part of it? Have the staff involved in courses relating to People, Families, Life, Community and the Environment in general, ever sat down and discussed their schemes with one another and considered areas of overlap or possible reinforcement? Are different departments all sending out pupils into infant schools and playgroups for varying kinds of community experience unaware of the pressure they are imposing on those working with young children? Where does the Home Economics department fit into this new course? Have Technical Studies been invited to join in? Who else could make a contribution? Who will do the actual teaching?

These and many other questions must be considered carefully well in advance of the course commencement. A minimum of six months is needed for planning and the ideal is nine months to one year.

It does seem that courses can either stand in their own right either as short courses of one term or one year with the two-year courses frequently being linked with a Mode 2 or Mode 3 CSE. The alternative is for them to form a well planned unit within a bigger scheme in, say, Community or Health Education.

Unfortunately, the question of the CSE examination is a controversial one and a number of people feel this work should not be tied to exam requirements. However, on the other side it can be argued that a carefully designed CSE based largely on continuous assessment (to fit the requirements of the examining boards there does have to be a written paper as well) covering the full breadth of the course ensures that quality is maintained. It is extremely important that these courses are well run and that the teaching is of the best possible standard because of the very nature of the work. It is, of course, true to say that this should apply to everything else in education!

It has been found that fifth and sixth years approach the work with a higher degree of involvement and this presumably is because they are that much older and therefore more concerned with their adult roles. As some girls will be mothers by seventeen the change of role is not far distant and can be seen to be relevant, if handled by a skilful teacher. Certainly the fourth year is the earliest desirable stage for starting this work.

Boys are definitely very interested in courses of this kind. In most cases straining at the leash to get into the adult world and be men the idea of considering their very important role as fathers appeals to them. This is true of all abilities. One 6th form 'A' level student who had taken part in a 12-week course in a boys school spoke eloquently on why he thought learning about being a parent was so important and said he thought the course should be integrated into sixth form general studies 'to broaden the education of every sixth former — something much needed nowadays.' Another said 'the course may not turn you into a marvellous parent but it is fun to do.'

Equally a fourth year boy, who could barely read, when visited in a playgroup said it was better than school and he wished he could be there all week. The playgroup leader spoke in glowing terms of his contribution. Discovering that he had something to give young children and there was something he enjoyed doing, for a change, could help this lad to achieve a sense of his own worth so that perhaps later he would take his role as a father seriously realising that he — and his wife — were his child's first teachers and, as such, people who have a very important job to do.

This involvement with young children leading to boys who had under-achieved steadily, changing and becoming interested, involved and responsible was noticed by the head of one boys school. Originally the boys had gone out as part of some community service but when the head observed their reactions and heard the views of the people in charge of the young children he decided that a school course on preparation for parenthood as well could really make a difference to the way his youngsters would approach their future.

How much time?

Time has been mentioned in terms of course duration but how much time per week? The most successful courses are those where a whole morning or whole afternoon have been allocated. Because so much of the course is concerned with various activities that are time consuming this enables them to run smoothly, eg practical experience with young children, visits to places of interest and relevance, practical activities within the home such as food for the family, home maintenance, making clothes for children, soft and wooden toy making. It is just possible to manage on split sessions but this often means asking the young people to use their lunch hour or break to return to school after being in a playgroup or day nursery, etc. Furthermore, they never see the *whole* routine of the group of young children and miss a great deal because barely have they settled in when it is time to return to school. Regarding the practical activities any Home Economics or Needlecraft or Technical Studies teacher will describe how unsatisfactory it is to be rushing through in just over an hour, both youngsters and teacher frequently winding up irritable as the pace just isn't right for them with its constant sense of rush.

And for those in urban areas visits which can be made are also time consuming because of travelling some distance to reach the desired objective.

If it is possible to have one additional period this can be used profitably for follow up discussion and individual studies, with the teacher abailable to help, but for most schools this does present too many problems in time tabling. Consequently this has to be squeezed into the morning or afternoon. If time tabling really is too difficult then it is better to postpone the commencement of the course. Starting with short and split sessions is courting disaster as the course will be purely theoretical and not brought to life with a whole variety of learning situations.

Which teachers will be involved?

There are no hard and fast rules in this one. Child Development courses are forming a new area of study and whilst all teachers should have acquired some knowledge through their training, others will have gained more through the field of practical experience in having their own children. It is interesting to note that there is a general recognition of the need to learn more about child development and in-service courses are well attended. One particularly good teacher when telling others about the course they ran in her school began by saying 'Well, I've had four children who are now grown up but when I started to teach this course I really felt there was an awful lot I needed to learn about child development.' Her view seems to be a typical one.

The very nature of these courses seems to demand that those who work on them have at least found their feet in their teaching role so that some or, rather more, experience is indicated.

It is also extremely important that people want to do the work and are not pushed into it for a variety of wrong reasons. Certainly it is necessary that teachers should realise that if they are parents they may well find themselves questioning things they did with their own children when they were young. And for everyone — teachers and pupils — childhood memories may be recalled which had long been forgotten. And possibly as well as being happy some will be unhappy. The main point about this is that people should be aware of the fact that it can happen but it may not necessarily do so.

A minimum of two teachers should work on the course. Carried entirely by one person what happens when he or she goes? Collapse of course? Or someone struggling valiantly to gather up the threads and only becoming really conversant with it all by the time a year has gone by? What happens to the pupils as a result?

Quite frequently the impetus for getting started will come from a Home Economics teacher because she will see the work as a natural extension of that concerned with Home and Family Living. And there is a historical connection as some study of mothercraft and the physical care of babies and toddlers has taken place in many Home Economics departments for the last fifty years of more.

Equally a Social Studies teacher or a Biologist with an interest in Health Education is often the person who gets going. But other disciplines do become involved particularly when the teachers are engaging in work of a broader nature and have moved away from their subject specialisms.

What really matters is that the skills of different people are used to support the course. No one teacher can be expected to know everything which is needed and the best courses use the expertise of several members of their staff.

Granted this can raise time table problems but where there is a will there's a way and problems of this kind can be overcome if staff relationships are sound.

What contribution can be made by people who work outside the school?

Careful planning will lead to an absolute wealth of experience from people who work with young children and in the community generally, being used to support Child Development courses.

Quite possibly the local health education officer and one of the local health visitors may already be familiar faces in the school. If so, then it is merely necessary to consult with them on where they fit into the course work. And if their services have not been used previously then who better for help with work on Family Health, Family Planning and Birth of a Baby? The function of the Family Health Centre can be explained by the health visitor and if the work she does with mothers, babies and young children is seen to be concerned with the child's total development then perhaps the importance of the preventitive work and early detection of defects will be recognised by the pupils. As stated earlier the National Child Development Study found that children from unskilled manual workers families were least often taken to 'toddler' clinics. There seems to be a marked drop off in attendance after the child is one year old. If, however, the health visitor is seen to be genuinely concerned for the welfare of her families then perhaps this rather depressing finding will be changed in the future as she does her work in school and becomes known and trusted as a local community worker.

Playgroup advisers to the Pre-School Play Groups Association, nursery/infant school headteachers can all be invited to make a contribution on how children learn through play and in any case the course will build up links with their particular areas of work. Furthermore, one of them will have to explain the different kinds of provisions for under fives. Where possible the matron of a day nursery should explain what Day Care means for young children.

The complexities of the Social Services departments need some unravelling and a social worker could help with this task and bring it all to a higher interest level with a few first hand illustrations of how people are helped to solve their problems.

Simple first aid and home nursing can be taught by people who have trained in both and can see that the pupils are given a short, down to earth, course in both, so that they are really capable of coping when required to do so.

Educational psychologists and other workers trained to help children could contribute to discussion groups.

Parents themselves should not be forgotten. One school invited a mother with playgroup experience in the Pre-School Play Groups Association to talk about this to the course. She has been present at every lesson ever since and plays a valuable supportive role. There is a strong case for trying to involve the mothers of the pupils in various aspects of the course work. Not only would this help to improve home/school relationships but the mothers would then understand the aims of the course and be less likely to offer conflicting advice to the young parents once the first child is born. It is a well known fact that the mother's influence over a daughter is a powerful one and does account for much repetition of practice originally carried on in the maternal home. The fact that so many mothers of older pupils work has rather prevented this idea being tried so far and perhaps a more practical experiment is having young mothers alongside older pupils in school with a programme geared to the needs of both.

The one thing which must be remembered when using anyone who has not trained as a teacher is that they should only be asked to speak for a short time and to rely on questions and discussion to elicit what the pupils want to know. However interested they may be in their job the concentration span of the pupils will soon waver if they talk for too long. An informal situation where a variety of work is progressing and pupils can talk to the person concerned in twos or threes is far better.

If the authority employs an advisory teacher who works on Child Development courses her role will be to try and provide information regarding contacts and resources. Some schools will invite her to join in the preliminary discussions when planning a course. As the courses get under way she may be able to offer some help if problems arise and she does draw teachers together in working parties so that they may exchange experiences and information, etc. Organising various forms of in-service training will also be part of her work.

Last, but by no means least the question of aims and objectives and how these are to be achieved in terms of content of course must be considered. In fact, they must be examined right from the beginning alongside everything else which has been mentioned so far.

3 Aims and objectives of courses

New schemes may be worked out by a group of teachers, who over a period of time, look at the needs and problems of their pupils and decide on the aims and content of the course. They may, or may not, include objectives as well.

Often the existence of a recommended scheme or one known to be working successfully in other schools will lead to an adapted version being designed for use in the school. If an examination is to be taken then the requirements for this will dominate the situation but even so, many teachers will still plan a scheme in considerable detail.

What does matter is that aims and objectives are well defined first, as getting deeply involved with the content can lead to being not too clear about the goals to be reached. This in its turn can lead to rather confused and poor learning situations for the pupils.

Large scale projects organised by outside bodies such as the Schools Council or the Nuffield Foundation produce programmes to be tried out in a specified number of schools. These involve teacher participation in the planning but the impetus comes from those outside the school working as project directors or in some consultative capacity.

Those who work for the Local Authority as Inspectors, Advisers, Advisory teachers and Wardens of Teachers Centres may be responsible for arousing the interest and enthusiasm of the teachers in the school for the new scheme. This may have taken place through some in-service training programme or through personal suggestion. Or it may be part of the job of an advisory teacher or warden of a teachers centre to become involved in the development of new schemes.

Designing good courses is an extremely difficult task and very few teachers have any special training for it. What is a 'good' course? By what criteria do we judge it?

In terms of the pupils obvious enjoyment and lack of boredom? In terms of their output of classwork, whatever that may be? In terms of passing an examination with good grades? In terms of the attitudes they are supposed to be acquiring (becoming good citizens, caring parents, considerate neighbours, etc). It's not easy to set out any course in terms of ultimate achievement, let alone measure its success rate and it's hardly surprising that many aims in education are regarded as being too vague. It's certainly easier to define an unsuccessful course because the one obvious factor will be total disinterest on the part of the pupils and every teacher knows what happens then.

A fairly common view of aims is that they are broad statements expressing what the teachers hope the pupils might achieve. Almost certainly they will be linked with values and standards.

Objectives are more precise and can be defined as foreseeable targets which can be reached by the pupils and thus should be a route to achievement of the aims. A whole school of thought in education believes that it is necessary to organise courses in a systematic way with clear objectives not only for each unit of work but for each lesson. In building up this ordered approach to learning the pupils knowledge will be tested frequently and through his own knowledge of his success he will be stimulated to learn more. If there is a failure then the teacher re-examines his approach and does not tackle new work until the failure to learn has been rectified.

Ralph Tyler says that education is a process of changing behaviour patterns of people but goes on to define behaviour in the broad sense as including thinking and feeling as well as overt actions.[1]

In any new course it will be plainly impossible to reach every possible objective and priorities will have to be sorted out.

These are general educational objectives which are valid for any course:

1 The ability to use knowledge to think out a problem, produce a possible solution and test it.
2 To be able to recognise when feelings or emotions are affecting rational argument.
3 To acquire new skills and use them efficiently.

In order to determine the specific objectives of the new course it is necessary to organise the content at the same time and the diagram on the facing page designed by Dr Michael Eraut may be helpful.

This very ordered and scientific approach towards curriculum design and the planning of new courses has a strong appeal for some teachers and less for others who for a variety of reasons prefer a more flexible approach. Much has been written on it and those interested would find it profitable to read further or attend courses on curriculum design promoted by centres of Educational Technology.

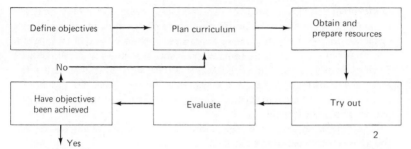

2

Nevertheless there is much to be said for an ordered approach to teaching and learning for there are times when courses strongly involved in contemporary life seem to lapse into 'providing of information sessions' through the use of speakers and films followed by teacher dominated discussion and it does become very questionable as to what is being achieved by the pupils.

To return, however, to aims. Few people would consciously recognise that the philosophy of education and the psychology of learning will affect their definition of aims. In fact, both must do so not only in terms of general educational principles and the values that are deemed necessary for a satisfying and effective life but in terms of what is possible in the learning process at different developmental levels.

Further, as they try to define aims various other factors will be at work, influencing them. For older pupils who are not being dominated by examination requirements and career prospects, meeting needs and learning how to cope with the problems of contemporary society loom large in the thinking of teachers. Undoubtedly this is because interest plays such a powerful part in motivation to learn. Also studies have shown a better transfer of learning when the pupil recognised the similarity between life situations and learning situations and also had practice in applying things learned in school to life outside it.[3] Subject specialisms will also have a bearing on how the aims are formulated.

So, what then are some possible aims for a child development course?

1 To provide an opportunity for the pupils to learn some facts about the main stages in a young child's emotional, intellectual, social and physical development.

2 To relate this knowledge to a study of family life, cultural patterns and community provision.

3 To consider the present role of the pupils as family members in relation to younger children and their future role and responsibilities as parents.

4 Through the study of child development and human relationships to enable the pupils to achieve an improved understanding of self and others, and so achieve more mature attitudes.

Quite obviously these aims are tremendously wide and highly ambitious. At best it can only be hoped that some of the mass of information available on those highly complex creatures — children — will be taught and that only some will be remembered and available for recall. Child Development is a disciplined academic study with continual research and new information becoming available all the time. So a school course has to be created within manageable terms and have simplified and attainable objectives.

The following are some suggestions for general objectives based on the aims which have been suggested.

By the end of the course the pupils should have learned that for the maximum optimal development within the first five years children need:

1   Parents with some knowledge of the developmental stages in young children, who will provide a stable and loving family situation so that the child will feel emotional security.

2   Communication with adults and brothers and sisters, through talking, being listened to, stories, nursery rhymes, finger plays, etc.

3   An enriched environment offering plenty of opportunity for play which is the child's means of learning about the world around him.

4   Nutrition and physical care of the highest possible standard.

If these objectives were partially reached by pupils there is perhaps some hope that their expectations as parents will be realistic. Not that this will be at all easy for them.

Parental role and emotional needs of children

Elizabeth Newson speaking as a parent and an expert in Child Development said 'it was comparatively simple for a parent to satisfy society's demands when the emphasis was on hygiene and affectionate firmness, and when the parental ethic included the dictum that mother knew best.

'It is much more difficult when parents are asked to recognise the child's emotional and egotistical needs as valid while still giving him a moral framework of principles — and moreover to present the whole in a democratic context which acknowledges that mother might not know best'[4]

She goes on to point out 'parents are chronically on the defensive over their parental role because not only is their responsibility limitless but also supremely personal. Their children are a walking testimonial or advertisement for the sort of people they are — which is fine so long as they are civilised and do them credit. But when young children choose the most indiscreet times for testing their parents' strength the parents are particularly vulnerable to situations which bring the child rearing process under public scrutiny.' After discussing in some detail the pressures which young children exert on their parents thus affecting their behaviour Elizabeth Newson says that she does not believe in parental consistency at all times. Her view is that human beings are inconsistent anyway and children must learn to live with this in the family circle. 'There with a permanent loving relationship the child comes to terms with variations in human behaviour such as being abstracted, moody or failing to understand and there is plenty of time for mistakes to be made and forgiven on both sides.'[5]

In our society the basic child rearing unit is the family and Michael Rutter says 'love and warmth are necessary in mothering. Where warmth in the family is lacking the child is more likely to develop deviant behaviour, particularly of an anti-social type. Warmth is an equally important factor in parent — parent and father — child relationships with respect to their influence on children's development. This implies that while warmth is a necessary part of mothering, it is not specific to mothering. Rather it appears that warmth is a vital element in all kinds of family (and perhaps also extra familial) relationships.'[6]

He also draws attention to the fact that studies of children in hospital or a residential nursery are nearly always considered as examples of separation from mother when in fact they consist of separation from mother and father and brothers and sisters and the home environment. In his view studies of the short term effects of paternal absence and the fathers influence are needed.

Furthermore it is in a young child's interest to encourage attachment to several people and not just one so that if one person is away another is present. If a child is used to short stays with friends and relatives in happy circumstances he is more likely to learn that separations are temporary and can be pleasant. Accordingly later unavoidable separations of an unhappy kind (such as hospitalisation of parent or child) are likely to be less traumatic.[7]

For future satisfactory social and emotional relationships it is necessary for bonds to be formed in early childhood. Generally these are with the mother or a mother substitute but should be with the father, too. A child who fails to form a bond with his father or any other male figure in early childhood may not be able to make a really close relationship with him later.

Bowlby's views are well known but according to Rutter have often been misinterpreted and wrongly used to support the notion that only twenty-four hours care day in and day out by the same person is good enough. He notes that Bowlby himself in 1958 and 1969 while pointing to the importance of the mother-child bond, and still regarding an attachment to one mother figure as vital says 'that it is an excellent plan to accustom babies and small children to being cared for now and then by someone else. Only in this way can mothers have the freedom to have some time released from child care to shop in peace or be with friends.'

He emphasised that care needs to be taken to ensure that alternative arrangements for mothering have regularity and continuity if the mother goes out to work.

Rutter says there is good evidence that children do not suffer when the mother goes out to work provided stable relationships and good care are provided by the mother substitute. This is an example of multiple mothering with one major mother figure sharing her task with the mother substitute. He does emphasise the need for high quality mothering and figures who remain the same during the child's early life (up to 4 or 5).[8]

Routine and stability are also necessary for young children. A chaotic existence arising through serious family disruption leads to a child whose behaviour shows evidence of stress — either withdrawal or destructive, aggressive behaviour. A study of Nurture Groups in London shows that the group provides a close, holding, mother-child relationship, experiences and behaviour management at a pre-school developmental level. Every task is broken down into stages. Various breaking techniques are built in — familiar and reassuring routines such as putting coats onto hangers. In these ways the children's experiences and behaviour are monitored as a mother would and psychological holding links are automatically built in . . . . Food is important in the groups for it embodies the mother-child relationship, affords maximum control and provides an opportunity to build in important learning experiences: holding back, waiting, sharing, taking turns and tolerating frustration.[9]

Consideration of what being a parent means before this stage in life has been reached will not be an easy part of the course. It is closely tied up with relationships and the attitudes people have towards one another — whether they are warm and caring, democratic, or cool, impersonal and authoritarian. In fact parental role and family membership will continually re-appear in virtually all aspects of the course content because one cannot study children in isolation from the factors which will influence them most.

Importance of communication and language development

There is much evidence to prove that lack of experience or stimulation has important deleterious affects on cognitive growth.[10] Children in institutions and some large families have been studied and found to be frequently retarded in language, general cognitive growth and scholastic attainment and are thus termed to be suffering from deprivation. But

Rutter says the effects on cognition appear to be due to a *lack* of stimulation rather than *loss*, so a more accurate term is privation.

'All forms of perceptual restriction may impede cognitive growth; different forms of restriction affect different intellectual skills. Probably the single most crucial factor in the development of verbal intelligence is the quality of the child's language environment.'[11]

'The vocabulary and concepts used by those around him are vital in providing a framework within which his own intellectual growth can take place. If this framework is bare or impoverished his development is likely to be slow; a rich framework of words and ideas will provide the food for more rapid growth. More advanced or abstract thought processes are clothed in more elaborate and highly structured language.'[12]

It has been suggested that because their contacts are more with other children rather than adults, that the children in a large family may have a language environment which is less rich and complex. However, it may be the clarity of the language environment, rather than its complexity which is the key variable. One study has suggested that children's verbal intellectual development is impaired in homes where there is a predominance of meaningless noise over meaningful communication. Another found that the presence of children tends to lead to a tumultuous clamour in which several people speak at once on different topics. Perhaps this kind of linguistic chaos makes language acquisition more difficult in large families.[13]

What certainly does matter is that babies and young children are conversed with by their parents and other adults in a one to one situation. Babies vocalise more when spoken to in a meaningful way and as the child's language development progresses he will need every opportunity to talk and listen to those around him. This does impose quite a demand on parents and particularly mothers.

Elizabeth Newson comments that the year between the third and fourth birthdays is characterised by rapid progress in language development closely allied with a steady broadening of the child's conceptual range. 'This is the period of 'How?' and 'Why?' . . . . the fact that he is becoming more adept at putting a string of connected thoughts into words has the effect of directing the adult's attention away from his earlier endearing idiosyncrasies and verbal mannerisms, and towards the *content* of the ideas which he is trying to communicate. This in turn stimulates the child to express himself more adequately in whole sentences or a series of sentences, which often now have an extremely complex grammatical structure. In short, real conversation becomes possible with a child of four and it is probably this more than any other development which makes him seem so much more of a personality. Most mothers welcome their child's conversation and find in it a source of deep pleasure to themselves; at the same time, many also find themselves flagging under the tirelessness of a child's continual chatter'.[14]

But not all mothers can cope with this need for conversation particularly if they have two or three young children and are unaware of the importance of language in determining the child's future success — or lack of it — in the educational system.

Eric Hawkins has suggested a widening of the present role of ante-natal and post-natal clinics to include responsibility for the linguistic and conceptual need of the baby, and his mother's education in carefully planned play and linguistic games. Referring to the excellent care provided by the Health Services for babies in the womb and at birth he considered that there should be a national effort to help overworked mums in coping with the most important intellectual achievement her children will ever undertake. And as part of this he considered that secondary school courses in mothercraft should be revised to give due place to language acquisition. He also spoke of the use of students and older secondary school pupils in language enrichment programmes for pre-school children. Because adult language can only be acquired from an adult this means one adult to every disadvantaged child and he foresaw use of young people for this purpose.[15]

Child's need for play

As well as richness of conversational interchange babies and young children must have an environment which provides stimulation. In other words there must be things around to see and do. Babies can have pictures on walls or mobiles to look at as they lie in their cots and toys to play with which will keep them interested and occupied. Not only will they be learning but they will be acquiring new skills as well and they do need adults to play with who talk at the same time.　As the child learns to walk and talk he needs more scope for play, 'Through play he learns about other people, he learns about objects through exploration, he learns about cause and effect, and time and space through experimentation and he learns to make and test hypotheses. He learns this through assimilating experience gained through play and by accommodating to new experience'.[16]

Joan Cass has said: 'Play is as necessary and important to a child as the food he eats, for it is the very breath of life to him, the reason for his existence and his assurance of immortality.'[17]

Adults have to make the conditions for young children to play — to give them space, playthings, time and a variety of experiences as part of their playing. It's not easy for mothers living in cramped conditions or in a tower block of flats to provide these opportunities. Lack of space means inevitable restriction on activity and where are playthings stored? A shopping expedition from a tower block of flats is a major performance and its hardly surprising that children in these families lack contact with people other than their mothers. They may only see the shop assistants and their fathers somewhat fleetingly for two or three days at a time. Children in rural areas can suffer the same isolation. One Director of Education said he was concerned because in his county the children often entered school neither able to speak nor walk properly. So much of their pre-school life is spent in a pram in the corner of a field while the mother works that their physical and intellectual development are often quite seriously impaired.[18]

So, playgroups offer a very real opportunity to compensate for a lack of play at home and at the same time give children the chance of social as well as emotional and intellectual development. They give mothers contact with other mothers and as they learn more about their children and play they also learn more about themselves. Furthermore they do get much needed breaks from their children. Mothers clubs can also perform a useful function for the mothers and younger children in a rather similar way but with more emphasis on socialisation.

Obviously nursery education for all under fives is the ideal and those parents whose children go to a nursery class or nursery school are in a fortunate position indeed. Not only is there a richness and width of experience in the good nursery class but there are skilled adults at hand ready to develop the interests of the children into a new learning experience.

Nevertheless there is no reason at all why mothers shouldn't be helped to make the most of the opportunities limited or otherwise for play in their homes and if they are *aware* of the importance of this for the child then there is no doubt that they will try, for they do want to do their best for their children.

Nutrition and physical care

In order to benefit fully from life around him in terms of both communication and play a child must be adequately nourished and healthy. Because standards of physical care are so much better today due to the preventitive and supportive work carried out by the Health Services it is all too easy to forget that this, too, must be emphasised.

There is evidence that certain infections in malnourished children can cause brain damage and early malnutrition will lead to a permanent reduction in the number of brain cells despite any subsequent nutritional improvement. A consequence of malnutrition is behavioural unresponsiveness. This means the child will have less opportunity to experience his environment and learn.[19]

'Severe under nutrition before two or three years of age, especially shortage in proteins and in the vitamins and minerals necessary for growth does indeed appear to cause lowered IQ. Seriously malnourished South African coloured children were some 20 IQ points lower than children of similar parents who were well fed.'[20]

Probably the most severe forms of malnutrition are less likely to be found in Britain today but there are still many families where money for food is in short supply and ignorance may lead to a wrong choice. A bottle fed baby may have the milk watered down by a mother who does not understand the implications of her action — or maybe thinks it won't matter seriously. The baby may be weaned on too many starchy foods and become large and fat. But what about brain development?

Nutritional studies must be well taught to adolescents and mothers, too, for good nutrition is vital in pregnancy and the first three years of life.

Good physical care means making full use of the excellent facilities provided by the National Health Service for babies and young children. In this way, early defects can be screened and acted upon, again enabling the child to take maximum advantage of his environment instead of being apparently retarded in some way or other.

These arguments should show how important the four general objectives stated earlier, are, in any Child Development course. They should be fundamental to any course although quite obviously there are other aspects which should be covered as well.

REFERENCES

1 Tyler, Ralph *Basic Principles of Curriculum and Instruction*, University of Chicago Press Ltd, London 1971

2 Eraut, Michael *Curriculum Innovation in Practice*, Edge Hill College of Education 1969

3 Tyler, Ralph *Basic Principles of Curriculum and Instruction*, University of Chicago Press Ltd, London 1971

4 & 5   Newson, Elizabeth 'On being a parent' *Where* February 1973

6 Rutter, Michael *Maternal Deprivation Reassessed*, Penguin 1972

7 *Ibid*

8 *Ibid*

9 Boxall, Marjorie 'Nurture Groups' *Concern,* National Children's Bureau, Summer 1973

10 Rutter, Michael *Maternal Deprivation Reassessed*, Penguin 1972

11 *Ibid*

12 Davie, Ronald, *et al From Birth to Seven,* Longman 1972

13 Rutter, Michael *Maternal Deprivation Reassessed*, Penguin 1972

14 Newson, John and Elizabeth *Four years old in an Urban Community*, Pelican 1970

15   Hawkins, Eric 'The importance of the early years', *Contact*. Pre-School Play Group Association, October 1971

16   Hoare, Carol 'The importance of play to the child', *How to form a Playgroup*, BBC Publications 1967

17   Cass, Joan *The Significance of Children's Play*, Batsford 1971

18   Crowe, Brenda *The Playgroup Movement,* George Allen and Unwin Limited 1973

19   Perkins, Stanley *Malnutrition*: A selected review of its effects on the learning and behaviour of children. International Journal of Early Childhood, World Organisation for Early Childhood Education Vol 5, No 2 1973

20   Brierley, John 'O to 8: The Growing Brain', *Trends in Education*, HMSO October 1973

4 A unit scheme and learning resources available

There is no blue print for Child Development courses and a number of approaches have been tried. The scheme set out in the diagram offers some suggestions of how the work can be approached in units. In this way a start can be made on any of them depending on how all the variables, which affect course content, are operating at the time. A group of fourth years will respond much better to the unit on Adolescence and themselves as a starter provided this has not been done to death elsewhere in the curriculum. As set out the scheme would take two years to cover thoroughly and if two more units were added — Children 5 — 13 years and Maturity and Old Age — would provide a comprehensive Human Development scheme.

Frequently work on the Family and Marriage will have been covered in Social Studies so care must be taken to reinforce this work if this is so and not to bore the pupils.

The vital emphasis on good relationships within and outside the family may not have been given overmuch consideration, however, so this could provide a fresh and reinforcing approach to setting the work on young children into its proper context.

A short course will have to concentrate on the four general objectives discussed in the previous chapter and the units on Conception and Birth, and Growth and Development of a baby and young child will ensure that this is so.

The following pages are set out with objectives for the pupils in each unit and associated learning resources, in the hope that this will be helpful to teachers. Much of the material has been tried out in schools where courses are under way but some has only been viewed and listed recently. In any case, the selection of material is a very personal matter and again, geared to the age, kind of pupil and length of course so teachers should choose what they feel is best for their school.

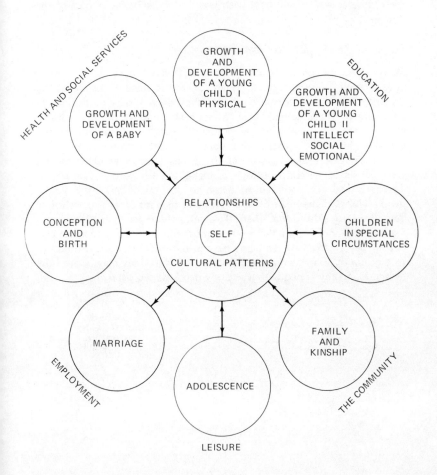

*Family and child studies
Unit scheme*

Play and language development will be covered more fully in the next chapter which will deal with practical experiences as part of the course.

People who contribute to a learning situation

Many of the people who have a contribution to make to the course have already been mentioned. Much concern is being expressed at the present time that secondary schools should be a part of the whole community. These courses offer a wonderful opportunity for forging closer bonds with community workers as they come into school and the pupils go out in to the experiences connected with their work.

It should be remembered that the pupils themselves often have a very considerable contribution to make to the group as a whole. Teachers who are prepared to listen to and encourage their young people will find they can offer a first hand account of an experience or demonstrate a skill to the others. This will only happen when the group feels settled and sure of the teacher whose role is that of supporter and encourager, in this case. One boy described his own learning difficulties to a group of sixth formers and had written very movingly about how he and his family coped with a severely handicapped sister.

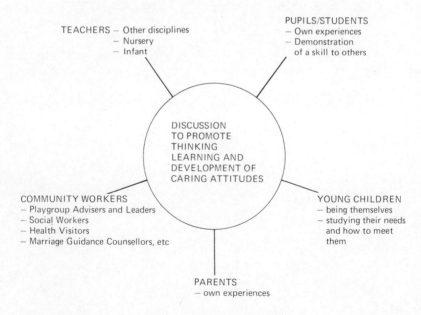

People who contribute to a learning situation
Child development courses

Frequently pupils have considerable skills in practical activities — toymaking, crochet, puppetry, simple musical instruments, cooking, games and songs from their own culture — and all these can be conveyed to the others.

An of course the contribution of young children to the course must not be forgotten . . . and more will be said on this in the next chapter.

Resources available for use in a learning situation

A technological society has brought a wide range of resources within easy reach of teachers provided money is available to buy enough items of basic equipment and buy or hire the resources themselves.

It is hardly necessary to quote the classic illustration of ordering a film, finding a room which blacks out, organising the film projector, getting the class there and then the projector breaks down. As more teachers are trained in the use of equipment and as more becomes available, thus reducing the strain on one or two overworked items, it is to be hoped that better things will happen.

First rate material is being produced all the time by TV and radio programmes, not only for schools and colleges of further education but for young parents too. Many of the TV programmes are put on film and can be hired but equally can be video-taped by schools and used when

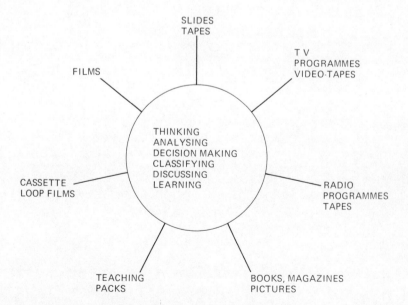

Resources available for use in a learning situation

required, under the copyright conditions. Similarly radio programmes can be taped and used. Films should be viewed beforehand and work sheets or tasks related to them designed, for use by the class.

Many loop films and slide/tape sequences are commercially produced but a school or college of further education could produce some of its own if cameras and portable tape recorders are available for the students to take out and use. Slide/tape sequences could be prepared quite easily. Loop films involve taking movies and need a staff member with some expertise in filming.

There are plenty of books for teachers and academic sixth formers but a real shortage exists of those written for the average fourth and fifth year pupil. This does entail preparation of handouts to summarise necessary information.

Teaching packs have nearly always been designed for use in specific courses and care should be taken to use them selectively and carefully.

Without work sheets and questionnaires throughout the course — and original written work — the teacher will have no means of checking that some learning has been taking place (even if much is forgotten). So, considerable time will be spent in preparation by anyone working on these courses.

ADOLESCENCE

Pupil/student objectives

Consider current relationships within and outside the family; examine the ways in which behaviour is affected by relationships.

Recognise importance of emotions and their effect on behaviour.

Know that self control, accepting responsibility, awareness of the needs of others and a caring concern for them are part of a life which is satisfying and contribute to the qualities of individual and communal life.

Identify factors which make for good physical health and understand effects of neglect and disease on the body and mind
   - right food (good nutrition and avoidance of obesity)
   - fresh air, exercise and sleep
   - freedom from social and contagious diseases (alcohol, smoking, drugs, VD, etc).

Have knowledge of the physiological effects of puberty.

ADOLESCENCE

Books for teachers

Children growing up   John Gabriel 1970,   University of London Press

Voyage Through Childhood into the Adult World   Eva A Frommer 1969   Pergamon

Childhood and Adolescence   J M Hadfield 1970   Penguin

Moral Education in the Secondary School   Peter McPhail *et al* 1972 Longman

Books for pupils (fourth and fifth years)

Courtship (Enquiries series)   Longman

Aggression (Enquiries series)   Longman

Drugs (Probe series)   SCM Press

His and Hers (Connexions series)   Penguin

For Better, for Worse (Connexions series)   Penguin

Relationships (Book plus 20 cards on myself, friends, the family, etc)   R Dingwall   Religious Education Press

So, now you know about VD   *Family Doctor* booklet

Teaching packs

You and Your Parents   Macmillan (Case studies and associated worksheets on relationships between young people and older generation)

Films

Half a Million Teenagers   Colour   16 mins   Concord NAVA

Gale is Dead   B & W   Colour   50 mins   Concord BBC Enterprises

Last Bus   B & W   30 mins   BBC Enterprises

The Butterflies   B & W   30 mins   BBC Enterprises

The Rebels   B & W   30 mins   BBC Enterprises

The Volunteers   B & W   30 mins   BBC Enterprises

The Game   B & W   30 mins Concord

Generations apart

A Week-end in Dorset   B & W   40 mins   BBC Enterprises

A village in Derbyshire   B & W   40 mins   BBC Enterprises

Two girls in Hampshire   B & W   40 mins   BBC Enterprises

Loop films

Points of departure series   Eothen Films Ltd
Love Story   113-117 Wardour Street
Engagement   London, W 1
Babysitter, etc

Social Relationships series *Young, Not So Young* *Relationships* *Social Interaction, etc*	Eothen Films Ltd
Patterns of Behaviour series *I like him, do you?* *Mother's Boy,* *Father's son, etc*	Encyclopaedia Britannica International 18-20 Lower Regent Street London, W 1

Tapes
The X factor (VD)
A Matter of Life (Family Planning)

Infotape Productions
59 Whitfield Street London, W 1

FAMILY AND KINSHIP

Pupil/student objectives

Compare and contrast family patterns in our society, including those of varying ethnic groups now living in Britain. Where possible, look at family life in other societies.

Recognise the role of parents and the role of children in the family. Consider how the changing role of the sexes may be affecting parental role.

Examine the role of other family members — brothers, sisters, aunts, uncles and grandparents — and consider the importance of their contribution to family life.

Identify social and other problems which affect family life:
  (i)   Unemployment, poor housing, long working hours, etc
  (ii) One parent
  (iii) Unsatisfactory relationships.

Make positive suggestions for the development of and maintaining of good, warm relationships within the family.

FAMILY AND KINSHIP

Books for teachers
The Family Mary Farmer 1970 Longman

The Symmetrical Family M Young and P Willmott 1973 Routledge and Kegan Paul

New Backgrounds R Oakley 1968 OUP

The Background of Immigrant Children Ivor Morrish 1971 Allen and Unwin

The Family Schools Council General Studies Project Longman and Penguin Limited. Michael Park. General Studies Project, King's Manor, York (Catalogue and 50 extra units of same material as in catalogue)

(*Suitable for sixth formers as well)

Books for pupils (fourth and fifth years)
Family Life Eric Lord Longman

Family Life (Enquiries series) Longman

Life in our Society K Lambert Nelson

The Family in the Community P Davidson Longman

Children (life of children from medieval times until today) D Kennedy 1971 Batsford

Teaching packs
Let's talk it over Work cards on (i) The Family (ii) The Home (iii) Local Environment Oliver and Boyd 05 002396 9

The Family Humanities Pack Schools Council Heinemann

Lifescape (Home, neighbourhood, community) Architectural Press 9-13 Queen Anne's Gate London, SW1 H9BY

Films
Four Families (life in India, France, Japan and Canada) B & W 60 mins Concord

The Family of Man Series (7 films on family living in England, New Guinea, Botswana and the Himalayas) B & W 30 mins BBC Enterprises

Where The Houses Used To Be B & W 60 mins Concord NAVA

MARRIAGE

Pupil/student objectives

Describe procedure for getting married in a church or registry office and explain the legal position of those who are married and those who have a common law marriage.

Explain the economic and financial aspects of marriage — cost of getting married, flat renting, house buying, furnishing, etc.

Consider the responsibilities of husbands and wives to each other — legally, morally, emotionally and in terms of relationships.

Identify problems which may lead to a marriage breakdown.

MARRIAGE

Books for teachers
Family and Marriage in Britain   R Fletcher 1967   Pelican
Captive Wife   H Gavron 1969   Pelican
(*Suitable for 6th form)

Books for pupils (4th and 5th years)
Becoming a Citizen   J Curry 1972   Harrap
    (New Generation series)
Money Matters (Looking Ahead series)   Longman

Teaching packs
Housing and You   Shelter Youth Education Programme
    86 Strand, WC2 ROEQ

Before You Get The Bird, Get The Cage (Slides on finding a home and
    buying a house) Shelter Youth Education

Films
Teenage Marriage   B & W   30 mins   BBC Enterprises
For Richer, for Poorer   B & W   30 mins   BBC Enterprises
Marriage Under Stress Series   B & W   ·30 mins   Concord
Children make a difference   B & W   30 mins   Concord
Breaking Point   B & W   30 mins   Concord
Put Asunder   B & W   30 mins   Concord
Family of Man Series   B & W   30 mins   BBC Enterprises

CONCEPTION AND BIRTH

Pupil/student objectives

Explain the human reproductive process and how conception takes place.

Compare different views on family planning and consider own position as an individual and member of a cultural group. Know methods currently available.

Recognise the importance of heredity in determining that every individual is unique.

Have a knowledge of the development of the embryo and how drugs, disease, smoking and the mother's emotional state can affect it.

Identify the importance of the following for the pregnant mother and explain why
   (i)   Good nutrition
   (ii) Ante-natal care
   (iii) Good health — mental and physical

Describe the father's role and suggest ways in which he can support the mother.

Have a knowledge of the general preparations which must be made for the baby, including preparation classes for childbirth and brief assessment of feeding methods.

Know how a baby is born and what effect the birth has on the mother, father, baby and its brothers and sisters.

CONCEPTION AND BIRTH

Books for teachers
Conception, Birth, Contraception   R Demarest, J Sciarra 1969
    Hodder & Stoughton
Everywoman — a gynaecological guide for life   D Llewellyn Jones
    1971   Faber
The Experience of Childbirth   Sheila Kitzinger 1967   Pelican

Books for pupils (4th and 5th years)
Population and Family Planning (Probe series) SCM Press
Birth of a baby   Marshall Cavendish
From baby to child   Marshall Cavendish
How life is created   Marshall Cavendish
First 9 months of life   G L Flanagan   Heinemann

Teaching Material
Charts on conception and birth   Cow & Gate Motherhood Bureau
    Guildford, Surrey
Publications of National Childbirth Trust

Films
Barnet (The Child)   Colour   50 mins   NAVA Concord
The First Days of Life   Colour   20 mins   NAVA Concord
Preparing for Sarah Parts 1 & 2   Colour   40 mins   Gottren Films
    113 Wardour Street London, W1V 4PJ

Slides & Loops
Human Reproduction and Birth 6 loops from Barnet (the Child)
    Ealint Scientific Limited Greycaine Road, Watford; WD2 4PW

How Your Life Began
Having a Baby   (Family Doctor Film strips)   Health Education Audio
    Visual 24 Bryanston Street London, W1

GROWTH AND DEVELOPMENT OF A BABY

Pupil/student objectives

Identify the physical and emotional needs of a very young baby and explain how to satisfy them.
— food, warmth, sleep, clothing, shelter, bond with mother (or mother substitute), bond with father.

Describe facilities offered by support services as part of post-natal care:
— Family Health Centre
— Family Doctor and Health Visitor
— Immunisation and Welfare foods
— Developmental checks.

List the different physical needs of an older baby, know how to meet them and know why they are important
— correct nutrition (healthy body and brain development)
— warmth and clothing
— protection from disease and accidents
— correct treatment of minor ailments
— exercise and fresh air and sleep.

Recognise importance of relationship between mother and baby, father and baby, older brothers and sisters and baby. Know why babies need a regular routine and need a loving and secure atmosphere for emotional needs to be satisfied.
State how fathers can play a part in caring for the baby and how they can help to reduce stress situations between mother and baby.

Explain the possible effects on the baby of the following separations:
— A series of baby minders
— Residential or day care
— Hospital (for baby of mother)
— Visits to relatives or friends while mother shops
— Regular mother substitute.

Describe how parents communicate positively with the baby and how this stimulates babbling and the beginnings of language. Importance of talking, singing, finger plays and nursing the baby.

Know how to provide an enriched environment for the baby so that he increases his co-ordinated skills through playing and inter-acting with adults — importance of playthings, simple toys and visual opportunities such as mobiles, pictures on the wall, etc. Recognise effects of over-stimulation.

Be able to list some of the main developmental stages in terms of *approximate* ages:

— sitting up, crawling, standing, walking, talking, etc, and know that over-high expectations on the part of parents are as bad for the child as a lack of encouragement to progress.

GROWTH AND DEVELOPMENT OF A BABY

Books for teachers

Maternal Deprivation Re-assessed M Rutter 1972 Penguin

Patterns of Infant Care in an Urban Community John and Elizabeth Newson 1965 Pelican

Voyage through Childhood into the Adult world Eva A Frommer 1969 Pergamon

Psychology of Childhood and Adolescence C I Sandstrom 1973 Pelican

Socialisation (Understanding Society) Units 6-9 1971 Open University Press

Children's Developmental Progress Mary Sheridan 1973 NFER

Babies and Young Children R and C Illingworth 1972 Churchill Livingstone

(NB Inevitably some of these books go beyond the stage of babyhood)
*Suitable for 6th form

Books for pupils (4th and 5th years)

Good Housekeeping Baby Book J Vosper Ebury Press

Better Homes Baby Book Collins

Child Care L Pitcairn Cambridge

Young Homemakers Book of Parentcraft A Creese Mills and Boon

Your Baby Mini Corgi

Your One Year Old Mini Corgi

Care and the Community (Health and Social Services) R Sawyer J White Ginn

Films

The Mother and Child   B & W   Colour   30 mins   BBC Enterprises
The Childwatchers   Colour   30 mins   Contemporary Films
   McGraw Hill
In the Beginning   B & W   20 mins   Concord
From Hand to Mouth   B & W   20 mins   Concord
Moving Off   B & W   20 mins   Concord
Their First Year   Colour   30 mins   Glaxo-Farley

Slides and Loops

Everyday Care for Your Baby   Colour slides   Camera Talks
Child Development   1 and 2 Colour slides (T305)   Camera Talks
Loop films on *Baby Care* (feeding, bathing, etc)   Eothen Films
   Limited, 103 Wardour Street London, W1V 4PJ

Safety for Your Baby (3 loops and 1 colour strip)   Camera Talks
The Work of the Health Visitor Colour slides   Medical Recording
   Service Foundation

GROWTH AND DEVELOPMENT OF A YOUNG CHILD I

Pupil/student objectives

Have a knowledge of child's physical development and how to meet his needs.

Be able to plan and prepare family meals — suitable for young children, showing knowledge of:
- correct nutrition and where help is needed in feeding
- choice of foods
- use of money, time and facilities available.

Consider how to clothe children bearing in mind suitability, cost, durability etc. Make clothes for children on a minimum budget.

Recognise a child's need for exercise and fresh air and know how to meet this in a heavily built up urban area — or when the mother is working.

Be able to deal with minor ailments and infectious diseases, including:
- taking a temperature
- nursing a fever
- giving drugs and medicine
- keeping a sick child occupied

Identify essential features of:
- diets for sick children
- home hygiene
- preparation for hospital treatment.

Examine the principle of good dental care:
- right foods
- cleaning teeth
- regular check-ups with dentist.

Describe how to make a home as safe as possible in order to prevent accidents
- protection from suffocation, burns and scalds, poisoning, electrocution, falls, etc
- know how to cope if there is a fire in the home

Identify danger areas for young children outside the home:
- roads and traffic
- strangers
- derelict sites and cars.

Study basic First Aid.

Be able to make a simple First Aid kit and be able to treat:
- unconsciousness and carry out mouth to mouth resuscitation
- shock
- cuts and grazes
- burns and scalds
- choking and poisoning
- fainting and fits
- foreign bodies and stings.

GROWTH AND DEVELOPMENT OF A YOUNG CHILD I

Books for teachers
Education and Physical Growth   J M Tanner   University of London Press

Children's Developmental Progress   Mary D Sheridan   NFER

*Elementary Science of Food   E M Hildreth   Allman

*Second Book of Food and Nutrition   D Wells and W Matthews Forbes

The Health and Welfare of the Immigrant Child   S Yudkin Community Relations Commission

*Suitable for 6th form

Books for pupils (4th and 5th year)
The Young Homemakers Guide to Nutrition   A Creese   Mills and Boon

The First Book of Nutrition   W Matthews and D Wells   Forbes

First Aid, British Red Cross Society   Junior Manual

Games & Play for the Sick Child   G and C Kay   Mini Corgi

Films
One Step at a Time   B & W Colour   30 mins   BBC Enterprises

A Tooth in Time   Colour   18 mins   Gibbs Oral Hygiene Service Hesketh House Portman Square, W1A 1DY

Where There's a Will (dental care)   Colour   28 mins   Gibbs Oral Hygiene Service

Slides, Loops, Strips
Hazard Spotting   slides   Camera Talks

Home Safety
  Medical Poisoning Accidents,   slides   Camera Talks
  The 12-15 month old
  The 2-3 year old
  The 3-4 year old
Safety and Oil Heaters   film strip   Diana Wyllie, 3 Park Road,
  Baker Street, London, NW1

What is Fire   Film strip   London Fire Protection Association,
  Aldemary House, Queen Street, EC4

Nursing the Sick Child   21 slides   15 min tape   Medical Recording
  Service Foundation
About Your Food
About Your Teeth (*Family Doctor* film strips)   Health Education
  Audio Visual, 24 Bryanston Street London, W1
Child safety (wall sheets)   RSPA

GROWTH AND DEVELOPMENT OF A YOUNG CHILD II

Pupil/student objectives

Have a knowledge of a young child's intellectual, emotional and social development and how to meet his needs.

Recognise importance of play and new experiences in a child's life.

Know that playing is a child's way of learning about the world around him. Recognise kinds and stages of play and know how to provide playthings including toys suitable for use in the home.

Describe play facilities outside the home.

Examine the provisions for the pre-school child and compare and contrast the differences in them:
- day nurseries
- nursery education
- play groups
- mothers clubs
- creches

Know the importance of communication in terms of being talked to, listened to, read to and sung with by adults, for satisfactory and full language development in a young child.

Identify experiences which lead a young child to development of aesthetic and creative appreciation:
- songs and music
- nature and living things
- tactile experiences, eg colour, shape, texture
- visits to places that offer an expansion of experience, eg sea and country

Recognise how the emotions (love, hate, jealousy, fear, guilt, etc) affect behaviour and how play can be a valuable outlet for feelings.

Compare and contrast ways in which children are taught to behave in a socially acceptable way. Know that child's age affects his understanding of right and wrong. Consider rewards and deterrents and whole question of discipline in the family.

Examine the differences between over-possessive, authoritarian, overpermissive and democratic parents and how their relationship with their children affects the child's behaviour.

Recognise the child's need for encouragement and praise, together with warm and positive parental attitudes. Also, his need to be accepted as an individual.

State ways in which a child learns to become independent for short periods from his parents and is encouraged to become more self-sufficient.

GROWTH AND DEVELOPMENT OF A YOUNG CHILD II

Books for teachers
Four Years Old in an Urban Community   John and Elizabeth Newson 1970 Pelican
Dibs: In Search of self   V Axeline   Pelican
Magic Years Selma Fraiberg 1971 Methuen (Paper and hard)
* *Reaching Out*   A Yardley 1971   Evans
Senses and Sensitivity   A Yardley 1971   Evans
Exploration and Language   A Yardley 1971   Evans
The New Childhood   E Wright 1972   Allan Wingate
The Growth and Development of Children   C Lee 1969   Longman
Child Care and Management   Patricia Edge 1971   Faber
*Suitable for 6th year

Books for pupils (4th and 5th year)
All you should know about your children   E Trimmer Marshall Cavendish
Your 2 year old   Mini Corgi
Your 3 year old   Mini Corgi
Your 4 year old   Mini Corgi
Your 5 year old   Mini Corgi

Teaching packs
Understanding Children   Childwall Project   E J Arnold
Note   Resources on Play and Communication are listed on pages 73 and 74

Films

Making Sense   B & W Colour   25 mins   BBC Enterprises
Power of Speech   B & W Colour   25 mins   BBC Enterprises
All in the Game   B & W   25 mins   BBC Enterprises
Children's Emotions   B & W   20 mins   Contemporary Films Ltd
Children's Fantasies   B & W   20 mins   Contemporary Films Ltd
God Bless Mummy   Colour   30 mins   Glaxo-Farley Foods

Ages & Stages Series

Terrible Twos and Trusting Threes   Colour   22 mins   Concord
Frustrating Fours and Fascinating Fives   Colour   22 mins   Concord
(old but regarded as good still for getting points over on development)

Strips (designed to be mounted as slides)

Priceless Play   Glaxo-Farley Foods
More Little Feet (how to cope with another child)

CHILDREN IN SPECIAL CIRCUMSTANCES

Pupil/student objectives

Consider how people cope with a physically or mentally handicapped child and the support services which exist to help them (local authority and voluntary organisations).

Identify the problems facing would-be adoptive parents and the child who is adopted.

Recognise the problems facing a single parent — finance, housing, employment, coping alone, etc.

Know the reasons why children may be in care (fostered or residential) and recognise the effort that is made to provide a good alternative home for them.

Examine the work of the Local Authority social workers and voluntary organisations NSPCC, Dr Barnado's, National Children's Home, etc. eg in caring for children and preventing cruelty or family break up.

CHILDREN IN SPECIAL CIRCUMSTANCES

Books for teachers

Young Children in Hospital J Robertson 1970 Tavistock Publications

Play in Hospital S Harvey A Hales-Tooke 1972 Faber

They Say My Child's Backward C H Jackson 1970 Nat Soc for Mentally Handicapped Children

Growing up Adopted Seglow, Kellmer, Pringle, Wedge 1972 NFER (result of National Children's Bureau Research)

Films

Your Child in Hospital (Parents & Children) B & W 25 mins BBC Enterprises

Going to Hospital with Mother B & W 40 mins Concord

Young Children in Brief Separation:
    Kate B & W 33 mins Concord
    Thomas B & W 35 mins Concord
    Jane B & W 37 mins Concord
    John B & W 45 mins Concord
    (careful preparation essential)

Today's Children (children in care) B & W 30 mins National Childrens Homes

Play and Development (Mental handicap) Colour 20 mins Concord

Slides

Toy Library for handicapped children Medical Recording Service Foundation

Who cares for Philip? (Fostering) Camera Talks

A Day in a Residential Nursery Camera Talks

5 Learning experiences relevant to the course, particularly with young children

A number of learning experiences exist through being involved in some kind of practical situation and these should be used as widely as possible. The most important of these is involvement with young children on a regular basis, generally in playgroups, day nurseries, nursery classes, etc.

Before considering this in detail, however, it would be as well to take a brief look at the other possiblilities which most teachers must be well aware of but perhaps haven't always considered as part of a Child Development course.

Family Health Centres, hospitals

Certainly girls ought to be familiar with the Health Visitor and her work at the Family Health Centre. Often a group are welcome and are shown all the facilities while the work is explained but, if it can be arranged, further visits by a couple of girls at a time to see the post natal clinic and help with the toddlers creche can help to build up good relationships and a realisation that the 'clinic' (in local parlance) is a supportive helping place for mothers. Bearing in mind that much of the teaching on the child's needs to parents is given via the Health Visitor and that many of the girls will be mothers by 17 or 18 it does matter that they should see the Family Health Centre as a place they will go to and *use* for through it much support is given to the family.

The FHC will offer the second reinforcing tier of teaching on children's needs and parental role after the school courses have been partially forgotten.

Local hospitals with a children's ward are often glad to have a couple of regular helpers and here boys or girls can contribute. Children who are physically handicapped and in hospital for long stays for a series of operations need play as much as anyone else and there are now playgroups in hospitals. It goes without saying that the young people must want to go and know what it will entail. Boys can make a particularly valuable contribution in toy making and mending and designing small pieces of wooden apparatus to make situations easier for the handicapped.

It is perhaps worth noting whilst on the subject of physical handicap that special schools are glad to have a couple of boys or girls and that where girls from one secondary school have been to a school for physically handicapped children they have all enjoyed their experience and deemed it worthwhile. They should have some alternative experience with normal children as well.

Toy shops, Mothercare shops, museums

By pre-arranging a visit beforehand small groups of pupils with a task to perform will be welcome. Studying how toys are made, examining safety points and costing them could lead to a new enthusiasm for making wooden toys a great deal more cheaply in the woodwork shop at school. Costing out the basic necessities for a new baby through visiting the Mothercare shop is a worthwhile economic exercise. If the local museum has a toy collection this is worth seeing if only to lead to thought and discussion — and perhaps research by the interested — on

PLAYGROUPS
NURSERY CLASSES
DAY NURSERIES
MOTHERS CLUBS

LOCAL AREA
— PLAY FACILITIES
— HOMES
— CHILD MINDERS

THROUGH OBSERVATIONS FINDING OUT AND MEETING NEEDS OF YOUNG CHILDREN CREATING AND MAKING AND HELPING

FAMILY HEALTH
CENTRE
HOSPITALS
SPECIAL SCHOOLS

PRACTICAL
CREATIVE SESSIONS
IN SCHOOL
MAKING   TOYS
          GARMENTS
          BOOKS
          MEALS
JUNK AND PAINT
SESSION
ROLE PLAY

MUSEUM
TOY SHOPS
MOTHERCARE SHOP

Practical experience leading to a learning situation
Child development courses

how children lived in the past. The fact that the toys which exist still, belonged to the well to do and that the children of the poor did not have a childhood as we know it to-day is not realised by many young people. This could lead to an interesting comparison with the life of children in more primitive cultures today.

Possibly schools in rural areas might be able to arrange such visits all on one day, to their nearest urban centre and with mixed classes set tasks related more particularly to each sex (boys and wooden toys, girls and costing out the necessities for the baby). Others may feel this isn't necessary and let mixed groups do it all — it depends somewhat on the maturity of the boys as to what they will take without embarrassment.

Local area and homes

A survey of all the facilities for under fives and a large map drawn up to show them would reveal all sorts of interesting things. In some city areas no real play areas within easy reach would emerge or long treks to the nearest Family Health Centre, playgroups, etc. A consideration of what is there and the effort needed to reach it is definitely valuable. It is a surprising fact that many city youngsters are extraordinarily ignorant of their own area and the facilities offered by numerous organisations. Some teaching on who is responsible for what is essential at this point but this can easily be a bore if not related to some practical exercise.

With the help of the local Health Visitor it may be possible to find mothers at home or child minders who are willing to have a girl or boy to give some help with the children. They have to be people who are trying to provide a reasonable range of play and language activities and who are warm and sympathetic to the children in their care as well as to the adolescent. Health Visitors know their families very well and probably are as good as anyone at making such a choice. In rural areas or areas where there are few other opportunities for experience with young children this is the only way of organising it. And it should be said that good child minders do exist and not all are bad.

Practical creative sessions in school

Many of the pupils taking a Child Development course have not had any Home Economics teaching or very little. Boys and girls should have an opportunity to make simple family meals together with positive teaching on the importance of correct nutrition.

There should be an opportunity for the making of soft and wooden toys and how this is worked out depends on the teachers and the group. Boys have made some first rate soft toys and girls some good wooden ones. Glove puppets are fun and can lead to language development exercises for the youngsters themselves in making up their own scripts for little plays for children.

Scrap books can be made for young children from coloured magazine pictures stuck on card (some system is needed eg things of one colour or things found in the home or outside) and stories can be written and illustrated. A surprising level of talent emerges in the latter.

Role play is one way of examining family relationships (particularly teenagers and parents) and the Schools Council Life Line material produced as part of the Moral Education in the secondary school project is helpful here.

And finally a session or two with thick paint, junk, clay and dough in a very unstructured way is not only creative but allows youngsters to work through their own very natural wish to play with these things in the nursery class or playgroup. If this is worked out of their systems beforehand then there is less likelihood of their taking over from under fives — which is a common error made by adults who do not realise that by doing this, they are interfering in and destroying the child's own creative activity.

Playgroups, nursery classes, day nurseries, mothers' clubs

Practical involvement with young children in an enriched environment forms one of the most important areas of a good Child Development course. *Preparation beforehand* is essential if the young person is to be in a learning situation and giving to it as well as receiving from it.

In recent years it has become common practice for many secondary schools to place pupils with under fives as part of their community experience or education. Usually there is no preparation beforehand.

This places a considerable onus on the adult in charge of the young children who finds herself explaining what is going on and how the young people can help. If she is interested in and sympathetic towards adolescents and can spare the time she finds herself giving information on children's needs and how they are met in the playgroup, nursery class etc, as well as giving plenty of praise and encouragement. It has been noted frequently that under these circumstances under-achieving boys and girls (often very nearly school refusers) flourish and develop a new maturity in this particular situation because there is something they can do, they become interested and they find it rewarding.

But — not everyone has the time or flair for giving this much attention to the teenagers and in any case they are employed primarily to meet the needs of under fives. So, the other side of the coin can be a couple of bored gum-chewing youngsters who come when they feel like it and aren't much help when they do, who may well steadfastly refuse all friendly offers made by the adult in charge.

It is, therefore, the responsibility of the secondary school to prepare their pupils carefully before they go to the Playgroups, Day Nurseries, etc, to organise on going work while they are there and to provide opportunities for discussion in school while the practical experience is going on. In this way everyone benefits all round and whilst the value of the informal teaching and sympathetic encouragement given by the adult in charge of the young children must never be under-estimated the secondary school is accepting its responsibility to teach its pupils some child development before they have practical experience; and is not asking quite so much of already busy and hard pressed people. But first, secondary school teachers must be convinced that Child Development matters. When they are, then perhaps it will form part of a community education course or be taught alongside it.

Preparations to be made by teachers

It is necessary to sort out the range of local provision for under 5s.

Playgroups

These are listed by the Social Services Department who have one person responsible for visiting them and seeing that statutory health regulations are met. The playgroup may be run under the auspices of the Pre-School Play Groups Association (PPA) in which case there will be a trained leader, a certain standard, parental involvement and an area organiser or adviser who is the person to contact. Save the Children Fund have run very good playgroups in deprived city areas but in future will be turning their attention to other work with children, gradually handing over the playgroup work to increased provision for nursery education. Frequently playgroups are run by mothers (often ex-teachers), often on a shoe string budget and therefore with rather limited equipment, but are nevertheless quite good. There are two situations which are not fruitful for secondary school pupils. One is something which calls itself a nursery generally with a rather quaint title. Usually run in a private house it is a child minding situation where young girls with no training and little knowledge of how to handle children are employed and the owner is never visible. The children will be quite disorganised and often aggressive.

The other calls itself a nursery school and may be in a private house. Here small children are taught in a rigid and old-fashioned way and are too quiet. Wax crayons, little pieces of paper, jigsaws and printed pictures will be readily visible but all the paraphernalia of the true play situation (sand, water, junk, paint, Wendy House, etc) will be missing.

Some teachers say that if their youngsters don't see these situations they will never know what is good or bad but exposing them to negative experiences does not seem right. Furthermore a very limited use of such places — simply because of placement shortage — held its own answers. The young people refused to go after a couple of visits. It is more positive to see that they know what is right for children and then they will be able to discriminate between the good and bad for themselves when they are parents. Certainly it is a depressing and salutory experience to visit such places and realise that people in good faith believe they are alright for their children.

Contact with all privately run playgroups is made individually by visiting (having obtained the list from the Social Services Department).

Some comprehensive schools with suitable facilities may decide to run their own playgroup. It should be stressed that this should be done primarily for the benefit of the under fives and not so they may be used as Child Development guinea pigs by the pupils. A trained leader should be employed by the Social Services Department and the playgroup run as any other with the children attending regularly, parental involvement, etc. Two pupils may then be in for each session but this doesn't cover very many pupils. However it helps and it may be an area where there are no other playgroups at all so it is doing a good turn to the nearby housing estate.

Younger brothers or sisters may be taken into the Home Economics flat for a meal to make a more realistic situation but real care and thought must be given to the question of taking very small children into a secondary school. It can be quite terrifying for a two year old to be dragged round this strange environment with all the noise and people everywhere and little thought is being given to the child. Furthermore, it negates all the teaching on trying to meet children's needs.

Day nurseries

These are run by the Social Services Department of the Local Authority. A person in charge of Day Care or just the Day Nurseries holding a senior management position must be contacted initially. If she or he agrees, then individual matrons are contacted and arrangements are made for the pupils. Day nurseries differ in their approach — some being rather rigid and super hygienic and others with much more play and free expression on the part of the children. A trained nursery nurse is usually in charge of each room with trainees working with her.

Nursery Classes and Nursery Schools

Nursery classes are attached to infant schools and each has a trained teacher in charge with assistants who are generally trained nursery nurses. The nursery school is built especially for under fives and has the same sort of provision on a larger scale and a head who is a trained nursery teacher. In a nursery class a wide range of learning experiences is offered to the children, often based skilfully on their interests at the time. Because there are not very many nursery schools they are heavily laden with college students and frequently cannot manage older secondary school pupils as well. This is also true of nursery classes but often the head will agree to have two pupils when they can fit them in because they believe that the education of future parents is of such importance. Heads of infant schools will also fit them in and this is helpful but it doesn't offer the same developmental range to be observed as with under fives.

Nursery centres

These consist of a nursery school and a day nursery under the one purpose built roof. They are staffed by trained nursery teachers and trained nursery nurses and have a dual function. At present there are only a few such centres in urban areas.

Mothers and toddlers' clubs

There are a growing number of such clubs, for playgroups don't take under threes and it makes a welcome break for the mothers to meet one another and chat and have a cup of tea while their children play. If, there are reasonable play facilities they offer a limited experience for pupils — and the interchange with young mothers should be helpful.

Miscellaneous

There are a variety of situations where toys are provided and one or two adult supervisors — the Out Patients Department of a large hospital, the Family Health Centre to name but two.

Their purpose is to take the pressure off mothers who can then see the doctor or attend to some shopping or other matters unencumbered with a small child or two. Some Family Health Centres call these Playgroups and in a sense they are but they do not have the same continuity and emphasis on learning through play as the children only attend when the mother needs this kind of help. Furthermore some FHC's run true playgroups so each situation has to be examined individually.

They offer useful experience to the pupils so long as they understand that they are child minding situations or creches, are not there too long and have experience of a very good playgroup or nursery class as well.

The most vital point about building up a number of placements for each secondary school is that in urban areas where there may be 3 or 4 large schools fairly close together *they don't overburden the under fives provision*. Teachers must check who else is using the placement. Only two pupils per session should be sent and it is not fair to expect the placement to cope with more than two secondary schools otherwise they will be overburdened particularly if they have parental involvement as well.

Points to note on preliminaries

1 The placement should be visited the term before the practical experience. The visit enables the teacher to explain to the person in charge (and others where necessary) that the pupils are taking part in a Child Development course and what preparation will have taken place. The name of the teacher, school address, and phone number should be left with the placement so they know who to contact. Privately run playgroups and nurseries may prove to be unsuitable when seen and in this case it is usually possible to retreat with honour saved all round by saying that 'one is making enquiries to see if they would have secondary pupils at some stage.'

To find time to do this essential visiting (it leads generally to splendid relationships being formed between the secondary school and the placement) it is essential to ask for day time release. This can often be achieved during the summer exam period as most courses start in the autumn.

2 A copy of the scheme should be left with the person in charge.

3 The fact that pupils will be expected to keep a diary of visits and make some observations on the children as well as be involved in the daily routine should be made clear.

4 A letter should be sent to parents asking for their permission for the pupils to attend practical placements. In this way, the school is safeguarded as insurance does not cover pupils visiting off site premises without teacher supervision. The letter should make it quite clear that the pupils will be on their own.

5 The pupils should be provided with a record card listing the name of the person in charge, the address and phone number of the placement. Attendances should be signed and apologies for unavoidable absence must be made beforehand by the pupils. Just not turning up is most disruptive to the relationship between the secondary school and the placement who understandably feel they are being 'used'.

6 A simple format for a report form should be designed so that a short report can be made on each pupil at the end of the practical experience.

7 It is most helpful for secondary school teachers to spend at least one or two sessions in a good nursery class, thus experiencing what their pupils will be doing.

8 It is advisable to file all the information on the placements so that other staff members involved in the course may have access to it.

9 Arrangements should also be made so that fares to and from placements are paid for by the school.

All this takes *time* and these courses cannot be mounted quickly.

Preparation for practical experience with under fives to be undertaken by teacher and pupils

Most people have found it necessary to get the pupils out on practical experience within half to one term of commencing the course. If delayed longer they become restless and keep asking 'When are we going out' and motivation begins to lessen. In a two-year course they will probably have about 12-18 sessions with young children, split into three half term blocks. In a one-year course there will possibly be two blocks of five sessions each. Overall this isn't very much but there is a lot of work to cover in the course and in any case the placements have to be used in a reasonable way. If a school has 60 pupils taking the course but only ever has 20 out in placements it only needs 10 placements which are then used steadily on the same days.

Assuming then that there is a term available before the pupils go out for their first practical experience it is absolutely essential to cover some of the work set out in the unit Growth and Development of a Young Child II. The general objectives referred to on page 56 should be met, albeit in a very limited way at this early stage.

Some teaching and learning must take place on a child's emotional needs in terms of loving and secure family relationships, his need for play and communication and good physical care, particularly safety at this point.

As an absolute minimum before going on practical experience pupils should know:

1 Why play is so important for young children.

2 About the different kinds of play (creative, imaginative, physical etc) and what they mean to the child.

3 The developmental stages in play (eg solitary, parallel and social play).

4 What playgroups and nursery education set out to do through seeing films, slides and loops and know the difference between all the provisions.

5 How to play an adult role with the under fives through having a talk with a nursery school teacher or playgroup adviser.

6 Why communication and language development are vital to young children.

7 How to tell a story and read a story with interest to children.

8 Some nursery rhymes and finger plays.

9 That books are essential for young children and, how to choose

suitable ones from the children's library as well as where to buy cheap Puffins and Storychair books.

In addition, as suggested earlier a session or two where they play with junk, paint, clay, etc, is not only helpful but therapeutic. The most awkward will gradually mellow and take part with interest and enthusiasm. Girls have been seen finger painting for twenty minutes non-stop and it has been commented on by teachers how normally noisy pupils become quiet, relaxed and peaceful in these sessions. Such sessions can take place in a playgroup after the children have gone but are often easier to organise in school. Needed are lots of newspapers for the floor and tables if classroom or a Home Economics room are used, a sink and hot water and detergent and cloths for clearing up. Powder paint, every kind of cardboard and box waste material, cream or yoghurt pots for paint mixing, thick flitches (hogs hair brushes), clay, ingredients for play dough and very strong glue for the junk creations, detergent or starch for finger painting. Then everyone, teachers included, has a marvellous time together but one word of warning to teachers — before trying to run such a session see how it is done in a nursery class or playgroup and then explain to the pupils that they are doing this at *their adult level* (they are *not* reverting to under five) in order to understand what children gain from such activities. Showing slides or a film of under fives engaged in the same activities at the same time goes down very well. For success such sessions have to be carefully prepared in advance and such skills as mixing paint to the correct consistency taught, because the pupils will then recognise that they can help in the preparatory work of the playgroup or nursery class.

Another thing pupils need help in, is observation. They find it incredibly difficult to make observations when out in the placements and this seems to be because no one has trained them in this skill. Perhaps they could make observations in the area, at home or in school and write these up. These then need discussing and maybe a few deliberate mistakes in the room contrived beforehand by the teacher might sharpen up their powers of observation. A very old game can be played where objects are placed on a table, observed for two minutes, then covered and everyone lists what they can remember. On uncovering each person checks his own list. It does help to make the memory more accurate and as the pupils will have to write up their observations after their visits to the placements it should be helpful.

Detailed studies of individual children to observe developmental progress are proving to be too difficult for the average pupil and, in addition, they are presenting teachers with problems in helping pupils to achieve a reasonably satisfactory result.

So, more general observations of what goes on week by week in the playgroup or nursery class linked with discussions in school on how the activities help the child or afford an outlet for feelings would seem to be more practical.

If sixth form pupils are going to study one or two children then some simple guide lines must be designed for them — physical, intellectual and social development are points which can be noted. Instruction in the use of cameras and tape recorders will be needed for everyone if these are to be available for them to use.

During practical experience

1 Some work sheets with simple observation tasks should be designed for the pupils.
2 These should have follow up discussions in school.
3 It is important for teachers to visit each pupil whilst out on practical experience and to further the relationship between the placement and the secondary school.
4 At the end the pupils should remember to thank the adults in charge for having them. It is a privilege and not a right for them to have this experience.

As the course progresses and the pupils return from their first round of practical experience more work on the child's intellectual development with particular emphasis on play and language should be carried out. A number of slides and loops on play can be linked with the work sheets so that the pupils can work in ones or twos on self directed activities reinforcing what knowledge they have acquired previously. A book which is invaluable for teachers is *The Significance of Children's Play* by Joan Cass and reading this should lead to all kinds of ideas developing.

Two of the many books on language are *Language and the Child* by M M Lewis and *Focus on Meaning* by Joan Tough. Both offer fundamental and vital information to teachers and neither is lengthy.

In fact, considerable work on language, relevant to the school situation is being carried out and in time this could become central to the content of a good Child Development course. Pupils should enjoy finding out about language. Poor readers have read children's books happily and without loss of dignity and have even developed a new enthusiasm for reading. They have worked in pairs and taped each other reading a story and have then made comments to try to improve performance. The writing or taping of a short and original story for children also highlights the importance of books read aloud to young children.

In a recent lecture given to teachers, Angela Hobsbaum[1] suggested that teachers should work on methods to make pupils aware of (i) how they sound (ii) the functions of language they encounter (iii) the variety of language they use. She suggested that pupils need to listen to adults talking to young children, children talking to adults and a child talking to another child; that such listening should be a critical as well as a pleasurable exercise. How much time is given to talking in the nursery school? How much respect is there for what children say? Listening to the language of a good mother or a good nursery teacher could enable the pupils to draw out some ideas for evaluating and appraising spoken language. She further suggested that if the pupils taped themselves initially and got friends to comment this would give practice and awareness in this quite difficult task.

Taping a whole variety of situations would lead to consideration of language form and style; the differences between the language which is spoken and written. The styles of intimate, casual, consultative, formal and frozen language, as discussed by Martin Joos in *The Five Clocks*, would make fascinating work for teachers and pupils together. The fact is that styles and situations affect the form which is used so that children may speak to the head teacher in an informal way and be told off for being rude.

In 1971 *Language in Use* was published. It is a book for English teachers and consists of 110 units each of which is an outline for a sequence of lessons. It is concerned with the relationship between pupils and their language. This relationship has two major aspects: what pupils should know about the nature and function of language and how they can extend their command of their own language in both speaking and writing.

If the English teacher can be enthused to put into practice much of the material in this project then this together with the work in the Child Development course could ensure that tomorrow's parents will have a new understanding of language and give their children so much more, particularly if their own linguistic development was limited.

By the time the second or third round of practical experience is reached the pupils will not only be highly involved in the work of the playgroup or nursery class or day nursery but they should have a useful contribution to make to this work. Repeated comments from adults in charge are that pupils who are taking a Child Development course are 'So much better' and 'More help' and that they like having them.

Undoubtedly the involvement with young children is of *key importance* to the success of the course for here all the theory on development and how to meet needs is actually seen in action. And

[1] Department of Child Development, Institute of Education, University of London.

who can fail to be touched by the influence of good nursery education, good playgroups and well trained nursery nurses who are offering an enriched environment to the children in their care?

PLAY

Books for the teacher
The Significance of Childrens Play   Joan Cass   1971   Batsford
Playing, Living and Learning   Vera Roberts   1971   Black
Pre-school Play   Kenneth Jameson and Pat Kidd   Studio Vista
The Playgroup Movement   Brenda Crowe 1973   Allen and Unwin
The Playgroup Book   Winn and Porcher 1967   Fontana
How to form a Playgroup 1967   BBC Publications
Mothers Help   S Dickinson 1972   Collins
Discovering with Young Children   Ash, Winn, Hutchinson 1971   Elek
Before Five   Scottish Education Dept HMSO
*Suitable for pupils

Films
As the Twig is Bent   B & W   20 mins   New Zealand House Film Library, 80 Haymarket, SW1
Before School   Colour   15 mins   Film Library County Hall Exeter, Devon
Looking at Playgroups   Colour   30 mins   Contemporary Films Ltd
Children Growing up Series:
All in the game   B & W   25 mins   BBC Enterprises

Parents and Children series
Toys in perspective   B & W   25 mins   BBC Enterprises
Please may I come tomorrow (Nursery education)   Colour   20 mins   Cygnet Films Ltd, Bushey Studios, Melbourne Road, Bushey, Herts WD2 3LN

Film strips and slides
Learning through Play (slides and strips) 1-3   Colour   Camera Talks
Priceless Play   Colour   Glaxo-Farley
Sensible Toys (strip)   Colour   Camera Talks

Cassette loop films
Learning through Play (Painting, Water, Domestic play, Dressing up, Sand, etc)   Camera Talks

Teaching packs
Childs Play — folders, colour slides, cassette tape   ILEA Media Resources Centre, Highbury Station Road, London, N1 1SB

LANGUAGE

Books for teachers
The Foundations of Language   A Wilkinson 1971   OUP
Language and learning   J Britton 1970   Pelican
Language and the child   M M Lewis 1969   NFER
Focus on Meaning   J Tough 1974   Allen and Unwin
Exploration and Language   A Yardley 1972   Evans
Language in Use (Schools Council Programme in Linguistics and English teaching).   P Doughty J Pearce G Thornton 1971   Edward Arnold
The Five Clocks   M Joos 1967   Harbinger USA

Films
Power of Speech   B & W   25 mins   BBC Enterprises
Getting Ready to Read   B & W   25 mins   BBC Enterprises

Teaching packs
Childs Talk — Work cards Colour slides Cassette tape   ILEA Media Resources Centre, Highbury Station Road N1 1SB

6 Evaluation and the future

Whatever kind of course is designed by the school, whether it is firmly structured or more flexible in approach, it will have to contain some methods of evaluation.

It is probable that in the future some courses will be designed which will have a system of evaluation built into them which will continue after the pupils have left school and become parents. Only by checking their attitudes in the early stages of the course, during it as it progresses and at the end and then later on, is it going to be possible to discover if any real behavioural changes have taken place. Equally, only this form of testing will check how much knowledge is retained from the school course and applied to the home situation with the new baby and later the young child.

All this will take years and a longitudinal project of a similar type to the one being carried out by Drs John and Elizabeth Newson at Nottingham University will be needed. However, all this lies far ahead at the present time and courses currently running rely on a variety of methods for testing the pupils knowledge.

Dr Ralph Tyler says 'If one wishes to find out what knowledge students have it may be easily obtained from paper and pencil tests if the students are able to express their ideas in writing, or can read and check off various item in a multiple response or other similar tests.'[1]

These tests do check what has been learned at the time and generally pupils respond well as they need some validation of success in order to progress. But they do take time for teachers to prepare and obviously have to be related to the ability of the pupils.

Original written work is a much more difficult proposition as it implies considerable thought and the expression of this through the written word is not easy for the less academic pupil. Yet, often teachers lean on this method heavily as a means of testing their pupils knowledge. For the pupil of above average ability this method offers some scope particularly when related to personal observation and experience as well as reading. Fundamental knowledge acquired in the course is applied and contributions made by academic sixth formers offer fascinating reading for the teachers concerned — and others, too.

But what of the pupil who struggles to write a few painfully inarticulate sentences as his original written work? Could he not tape his thoughts? Some poor writers can speak fluently. But if hampered by verbal inadequacy as well, then perhaps it is best to concentrate on simple questionnaires and multiple choice tests. Often this boy or girl will prove to be good with the under fives and the right adult; and through the teacher's observation of him or her in this situation here is another method of assessment of how much knowledge is being applied.

One such girl unaware of the fact that her teacher had slipped into the busy play group told a story brilliantly and successfully to a small group of children. Her teacher was amazed and delighted to discover that in this situation she was performing quite differently to her usual inarticulate and withdrawn manner in school.

Records of visits to the under five situation and a child study are another way of checking if learning is taking place through the observation of young children.

The making of toys, children's clothes, doing home maintenance jobs and preparing meals are all tasks which enable the pupil — particularly the less academic one — to show evidence of interests and skills.

Dr Tyler approves of all these methods and says 'since evaluation involves getting evidence about behaviour changes in the students, any valid evidence about behaviours that are desired as educational objectives provides an appropriate method of evaluation.'[2]

A CSE examination course should have all these methods of testing built into it as part of the course design but should be heavily weighted on the side of *continuous* assessment in order to give the less academic a fair chance all round over a period of time.

In a school which was recently assessed by the Moderator of a CSE Examination Board where a final display of work — or evidence of work — carried out in the course was set up, two teachers independently made the same observation. Namely that several of the pupils who earlier had tended to drift through the course had suddenly been motivated to make a tremendous effort to finish work and make and collect things to make a really attractive display. For the pupils the display of work had suddenly come into their line of vision as a foreseeable goal and something to aim for because they knew someone was coming to look at their work. How often has the teacher of any subject with a practical test with a visiting assessor or examiner seen this last minute surge of effort. (So often and sadly, too late for an appreciable difference in exam results.) Distant goals in education seem such a long way off for many young people that they seem unreal and it is only the goal which lies just within reach that holds any relevance.

Family child rearing patterns are responsible for many young people not being able to endure long periods of postponed satisfaction in long term interests.

Concluding a paper on 'Styles of Child rearing and their implications for early school experiences' Dr Elizabeth Newson said:

'By explaining control and discipline in terms of mutual responsibilities, middle class mothers set the scene for what will be consistent training in the values attached to long-term aims, long-term rewards, long-term responsibilities; this has enormous implications for a child who is to embark on a process of education which is to last many years. Working class mothers, by setting control in terms of authority and paying for bad behaviour, do not demand long term responsibility but rather induce a short term outlook for get-what-you-can and pay-if-you-must. This makes it difficult for the child to cope with postponed rewards, and is counter productive for the values which produce a person who is education oriented..'[3]

So it is very important indeed that objectives are tested continuously throughout the course and that there is a steady build up of achievement towards the final total. Perhaps this seems a rather obvious thing to say for it is fundamental to good education. But there is a risk that in a Child Development course, particularly if it is not linked to a CSE examination, there will be a variety of learning experiences offered which lead to insufficient involvement and effort by the pupils. For example, there may be some good films shown, an interesting talk or two from outside experts, visits to play groups, etc, and in the end the teacher is working extremely hard to provide all this for the class who take part passively and at the end of it all, probably remember very little. They must be tested, they must make contributions of their own, they must be put into situations where they think for themselves through pupil centred activities (this is essential anyway in a mixed ability group).

Only through deep involvement will these young people find the whole course rewarding and something which enables them to be successful. Because of the very nature of the work involved, this kind of course cannot afford to be associated with failure. It is far better to run a simple course with relatively few objectives which can be reached, rather than a wide one with so many goals that few, if any are ever reached.

Once a course of this kind is launched and is running well there will be considerable interest in it and a readiness to try to get into the next session if it is an option. In one school which had 24 girls in a sixth form group there were 70 applicants for the same number of places the following year. It is interesting to note that in the Schools Council Enquiry on Young Leavers in 1968 78% thought things to do with running a home and bringing up children were very important. Similarly 92% of their mothers rated school subjects related to these topics as very important for girls but only 17% rated them very high for boys[4]

So, the interest in taking part in these courses is likely to be there and at any stage from 14 to 15 years onwards there is a real chance of effecting change. After the exhausting phase (for all concerned) of early puberty the youngster is questioning his role in life. In childhood the parents dominate the child's world.

David Hargreaves says 'As the child takes the attitudes of his parents to himself, he begins to acquire a conception of the role of the child. His parents expect certain forms of behaviour from him and when he conforms to these expectations he is rewarded by them either materially or with love and approval. If he deviates from these expectations he is punished. The child is learning how a child should behave. He is learning the role of a *child* in relation to his *parents* and then more specifically the role of a *son* in relation to his *mother* and *father.* Concomitant with his understanding of the son role is his understanding of the role of mothers and fathers.'[5]

So, the child's view of the world initially is based upon the knowledge, beliefs and values he acquires from his parents and family. But as his social world expands and he starts to perform a number of roles so he comes under the influence of other groups. 'Every new group the child enters — the school, the gang, the club, the job, the marriage — bring new significant others to exert their influence, just as they bring new roles to be learned. Often there will be relatively little conflict between the old and new in the transitions between groups and roles . . . but every transition involves some degree of change . . .'[6]

So by mid-adolescence the youngster is engaged in a period of great potential change. Eva Frommer says 'that the epoch of puberty and adolescence can be regarded as a recapitulation and transformation of the first epoch of life. It provides a second chance.'[7]

She points out that 16 and 17 year olds have a deep rooted longing for confirmation of their role in the world. They may outwardly rebel and apparently reject the standards of their elders but inwardly question 'What part am I to play in this world? What is my contribution to be to human society? Will it be rejected? Will I be redundant, not only in work but also in all else that I have it in me to give? Will anyone want me now that I have grown beyond my parental home?'[8]

This is the time when it is vital to have the right adolescent/adult relationships and even more so in a course where human relationships and child development studies are inextricably mixed. A survey of 800 adolescents for the Schools Council Project in Moral Education showed that adolescents wanted:

   (i) a situation where adults allow 'reasonable' freedom

 (ii) help with problems or difficulties after inviting the adult to give it. Taking over a situation and doing what was needed for the boy or girl was less welcome

 (ii) quiet efficiency in adults who are teaching, handling awkward situations, etc

(iv) adults who listen, try to understand and are tactful and don't impose formality for the sake of preserving distance

 (v) adults who are predictably considerate not in the sense that they always do the same thing but in the sense that they react in the same generally considerate way to others at different times.[9]

All this comes back to parental role as well as teacher role. The sensitive and sympathetic teacher working in these courses will, in fact, be acting in a parental role to the group. By his or her attitudes and values and teaching on meeting the needs of young children some change will be effected in the young people who up to this point will only have been influenced by their own upbringing and the family attitudes in this matter. So it is not unreasonable to hope that those from homes where the child rearing was short on communication and play may at least try to provide greater opportunities for both with their own children.

Rutter, Argyle and Banks and Finlayson have all pointed out the importance of love and warmth — as well as control — in the parent/child interaction, this being given wisely and with great skill.[10]

It is therefore equally important that the educational process in a Child Development course should centre on a considerate style of life between the teachers and the group and all the others who are involved, too. The Schools Council Moral Education project offers a wealth of material which can be used in this context but it must be remembered that in the long run it is the attitudes of the adults which will count the most. If they practice what they preach then they will be heeded and it should not be forgotten that a sense of humour is worth a great deal.

McPhail, Ungoed-Thomas and Chapman say that 'An education in the considerate style of life is not one which relies exclusively on rationally persuading schoolboys and schoolgirls to accept that it is right to treat others as ends in themselves, to treat them with consideration. It is not even that which goes further and educates the children in what consideration is in many situations. Effective education is learning to care; also and most important, it demonstrates the considerate style of life in action and motivates children to adopt it because it is a rewarding and attractive way in which to live. We know this can work. We have seen it happen.'[11]

So it is to be hoped that our young people will learn to be more caring towards people. For implicit in this is a reasonable chance that they will try to develop a loving, warm, and encouraging atmosphere for the upbringing of their children — so vital for the child's self-image and future success in school and life generally.

By now it must be very apparent that two factors loom large for these courses to be successful. One is teacher preparation and the other is time. This kind of work is time consuming but deeply rewarding and well worth all the effort. Not only does it need time on the school time-table allocated generously but it will take many hours of time in extra training and preparation of resource material and methods of testing and evaluating. Also, each individual in the group will need time — not easy when people have so many jobs to do and there is so much pressure in a large school.

What kind of preparation will have to be made by teachers?

Reading on Child Development and watching TV programmes on parental role and children can be carried out when convenient but some must take place before the course is launched. Some study of child rearing patterns and how they affect children is necessary. The National Child Development Study stated that all teachers should engage in this as part of their training.[12]

In multi-cultural areas it is necessary to read as much as possible on the way of life of the different groups but to date little has been published on child rearing. There is, however, some evidence that West Indians need help in understanding the value of play and adult/child interaction of the pre-school period.[13]

Some study of inter-personal relations and group dynamics seems to be fundamental to the success of the course. The whole question of how people interact becomes quite absorbing when linked with the different family approaches to life. Discussion is a technique which needs using well in the courses and surprisingly it can still be wrongly handled with the pupils sprawled behind desks and not in a face to face circle with the adult. Furthermore, teachers get so used to talking they sometimes forget to listen and dominate the discussion thus preventing their youngsters from making their very necessary contributions.

It is always helpful to join with others when engaged in preparing for or running a new course because this offers an opportunity to discuss worries and problems. Some local authorities will have programmes of in-service training run by their advisory services. But other areas will perhaps have only one school starting up a course miles away from a neighbour doing the same thing and no in-service programme. Could a small group of interested people get together and link up with the nursery or infant adviser or a primary school head or an educational psychologist or a lecturer in the college of education or university? Provided the person concerned believes in the value of these courses and has the training and background in some aspect of young children's needs this should be most helpful.

Some form of group exercise is needed at some stage for people will be daunted and overwhelmed by the massive task which lies ahead if they are not supported by others. And there are numerous people all round who can offer something as well as the afore-mentioned. What about the pre-school playgroup adviser, a social worker, a family doctor (if he can spare the time) a health visitor, an interested parent who may be qualified in sociology, social psychology or psychotherapy?

The teacher preparation must be supported by the expertise of all those whose daily work brings them into contact with children. Those working in these courses must use the skills of others and there will be an obvious strength in a united inter-disciplinary team working on the course. And, of course, the experience of many teachers as parents themselves is an additional strength.

The role of the parent is not an easy one but the family continues to hold its own in our technological society. As Young and Willmott point out 'as the disadvantages of the new industrial and impersonal society have become more pronounced, so has the family become more prized for its power to counteract them. [14]

Given help by a home visitor parents who had not realised the importance of their role as the first teachers of their children began to change their attitudes and recognise that they could teach their children from an early age. Fathers were particularly fascinated by this idea and one man who had done badly himself at school remarked that while children were young 'all you can do is play with them'. He had bought and encouraged his son to do jigsaws from an early age as this was one of his own hobbies, yet he never realised that 'playing' was 'learning'. He was a natural teacher for his children and by realising the importance of his role he was even more encouraged to carry on. [15]

Parents do care about their children and are anxious for them to do well sometimes having expectations which are unrealistically high — or conversely — too low. Courses in Child Development and Human Relationships will offer very considerable preparation for future parental role which is long overdue. Once people appreciate how children learn and there is an interaction between the secondary school and the under fives in the area, as well as the community generally, then by the time they have children some of the barriers at present existing between families and the schools will start to break down. The lack of understanding on what the school is trying to do will no longer be there for the parents will recognise their own active involvement in the child's education. There is hope for the future that young children will arrive at school better able to benefit from what is offered. Not only will they have parental backing involved in a loving, caring way for their progress but their parents will recognise the value of their contribution — and in school where possible — thus achieving feelings of greater self worth.

Courses in Child Development should lead to the intellectual potential of the individual being developed, so that intellect and judgment can be directed responsibly towards people and situations. There must be an acceptance of personal responsibility, a sense of achievement, an ability to carry authority, and a caring, considerate style of life leading to a steady growth in maturity.

Courses of this kind will make a heavy demand on staff, resources, money, and time but they must be of the highest quality for within them can lie the future of the next generation.

REFERENCES

1 Tyler, Ralph W, *Basic Principles of Curriculum and Instruction*. The University of Chicago Press, London 1971 (USA 1949)
2 *Ibid*
3 Newson Elizabeth *Styles of Child Rearing and their Implications for Early School Experiences* OMEP Research Seminar 1972
4 Schools Council Enquiry *Young School Leavers*, HMSO 1968
5 Hargreaves David H, *Interpersonal Realtions and Education* Routledge and Kegan Paul 1972
6 *Ibid*
7 Frommer, Eva *A Voyage Through Childhood into the Adult World*, Pergamon Press 1969
8 *Ibid*
9 McPhail Peter, Ungoed-Thomas J.R, Chapman Hilary, *Moral Education in the Secondary School*, Longmans 1972
10 Rutter Michael, *Maternal Deprivation Re-assessed*, Penguin 1972
Argyle Michael,*The Psychology of Interpersonal Behaviour*, Pelican 1967
Banks Olive and Finlayson Douglas,*Success and Failure in the Secondary School*, Methuen 1973
11 McPhail Peter, *et al Moral Education in the Secondary School*, Longmans 1972
12 Davie Ronald, *et al From Birth to Seven*, Longmans 1972
13 Rutter Michael, *et al The Children of West Indian Immigrants*, New Society 14 March 1974
Pollak Margaret, *Three Year Olds in South London*, Heinemann, Spastics International 1973
14 Young Michael, Willmott Peter, *The Symmetrical Family*, Routledge and Kegan Paul 1973
15 Educational Priority – Vol 1 HMSO 1972 (edited by A H Halsey)

Books for teachers

Some more books which are not listed in Chapter 4 but offer useful background reading are suggested here.

The process of development and interpersonal relationships

Child Care and the Growth of Love John Bowlby 1953 Pelican
The Child, the Family and the Outside World D W Winnicott 1964 Pelican
Psychology of Developing Children P M Pickard 1970 Longman (Hardback and paperback)
Human Development Eric Rayner 1972 Allen and Unwin (Hardback and paperback)
Childhood A Sociological Perspective M D Shipman 1972 NFER
The Integrity of the Personality Anthony Storr 1963 Pelican
The psychology of Interpersonal Behaviour Michael Argyle 1967 Pelican
Interpersonal Relations and Education David Hargreaves 1972 Routledge and Kegan Paul
Human Groups W J H Sprott Pelican

The multi-cultural society

West Indian Children in London Katrin Fitzherbert 1967 Bell
Rampal and his family The story of an Immigrant U Sharma 1971 Collins
Sikh Children in Britain Alan James 1974 OUP

The underachieving child

Children in Distress A Clegg and B Megson 1968 Penguin Education
Backwardness and Educational Failure R Gulliford 1969 NFER

General Films Teachers and 6th form
If at first you don't succeed ..... you don't succeed B & W 50 mins BBC Enterprises
The Red House B & W 25 mins BBC Enterprises
In Search of Identity (West Indians and their problems) B & W 25 mins BBC Enterprises

Children Thinking series
Discovering the World　B & W　30 mins　BBC Enterprises
The Moon Follows Me
'Cos its Naughty
Playing the Game

The Springs of Learning series
The Early Years　B & W　30 mins　NAVA
Babyhood　B & W　30 mins　NAVA
Rising Two　B & W　30 mins　NAVA
Ideas of Their Own　B & W　30 mins　NAVA
Playing Together　B & W　30 mins　NAVA
The Pre-School Child　B & W　30 mins　NAVA

Slide and Tape Sequences (Teaching training)
Dr Mary Sheridan
1 *Stepping Stones of Development in Babies and Young Children*
    Medical Recording Service Foundation　64 slides　30 minute tape
2 *Development of Skill and Ability in the Normal Baby*　Medical
    Recording Service Foundation　48 slides　37 minute tape
3 *Development of Communication in Young Children*　Medical Rec-
    ording Service Foundation　48 slides　43 minute tape
Dr Elizabeth Newson
1 *The Innocent Eye* (Intellectual development as seen in children's
    paintings of their mothers)　Medical Recording Service Foundation
    46 slides　30 minute tape
Dr John Newson
1 *Playthings for the Handicapped Child*　Medical Recording Service
    Foundation　58 slides　38 minute tape

RESOURCES I

Films can be obtained from the following sources. Some may be obtained from County Film Libraries and Health Education offices.
BBC Enterprises Film Hire
25 The Burroughs
Hendon, London, NW4   Tel: 01-202 5342 and 7134
Free catalogue. Range of films on the family and child development.
Hire charges from £4.00

Concord Films Council Ltd
Nacton
Ipswich, Suffolk
IP10 OJ2   Tel:0473 76012
Catalogue 25p inc postage. Wide range of films on personal relationships, the family and child development

Contemporary Films Limited
55 Greek Street
London, W1V 6DB   Tel: 01-734 4901
Catalogue of McGraw-Hill films available. Limited number of films available, made in USA.

Educational Foundation for Visual Aids
33 Queen Anne Street
London, W1M OAL   Tel: 01-636 5742
Produce catalogues listing audio-visual material from many sources under subject headings. Most items listed can be hired from the N.A.V.A. Library.
Part 6 (Hygiene and Health, Teacher education) 87p inc postage

Glaxo-Farley Foods Film Library
Publicity Services
Glaxo Laboratories Limited
Greenford, UB6 3434   Tel: 01-422 3434
Free information on films, filmstrips available

National Audio-Visual Aids Library
Paxton Place
Gypsy Road; SE 27   Tel: 01-670 4247

National Children's Home
85 Highbury Park
London N5 1UD   Tel: 01-226 2033
Limited number of films available showing work with children in care

Unilever Film Library
Unilever House
Blackfriars, London   Tel: 01-353 7474
Free catalogue. Films on dental health from Gibbs Oral Hygiene
Service

Film Strips, Slides and Loops
Camera Talks Limited
31 North Row
London W1R 2EN   Tel: 01-493 2761

Ealing Scientific Limited
Greycaine Road
Watford
WO2 4PW   Tel: 92 22272

Eothen Films (International) Limited
113-117 Wardour Street
London W1V 4PJ   Tel: 01-734 9743

Health Education Audio Visual
24 Bryanston Street
London, W1   Tel: 01-486 3755
(*Family Doctor* filmstrips)

Medical Recording Service Foundation
Kitts Croft
Writtle
Chelmsford, Essex   Tel: 0245 421475

RESOURCES II

British Association for Early Childhood Education
Montgomery Hall
Kennington Oval, SE 11   Tel: 01-582 8744
Formerly the Nursery School Association. Publish many useful booklets and leaflets on the development of young children

Family Doctor Publications
47-51 Chalton Street
London NW1 LHT   Tel: 01-387 9721
Publish many booklets which are aimed to help parents. Could be used selectively with 6th formers. Also publish film strips (see Resources I)

Family Planning Association
27-35 Mortimer Street
London, W1A 4QW   Tel: 01-636 7866
Publish useful material and run courses for teachers.

Gibbs Oral Hygiene Service
Hesketh House
Portman Square
London, W1A 1DY   Tel: 01-486 1200
Publish a number of leaflets, booklets and posters on dental health. Also produce films available through Unilever (see Resources I)

Health Education Council
78 New Oxford Street
London, WC1A 1AH   Tel: 01-637 1881
Produce lists of material availabe for Health Education. Publish own leaflets and posters.

Pre-School Play Group Association
Alford House
Aveline Street
London, SE 11   Tel: 01-582 8871
Annual subscription for an individual is £3.50 from 1st October. Membership includes 10 copies of *Contact* which is a very useful magazine for playgroup leaders and parents.
Many other excellent publications including a termly newspaper *Playgroup News* which could be purchased and used by pupils.

National Childbirth Trust
7 Queensborough Terrace
London, W2 3TB   Tel: 01-229 9319
Various publications on prepared childbirth. A catalogue of teaching aids is available and Study Days are held on new visual aids.

National Children's Bureau
8 Wakley Street
London, EC1 V7QE   Tel: 01-278 9441
Annual membership for an individual is £2.10. A journal *Concern* is received 3 times a year plus other useful information about publications and research findings on children. Members can ask for the film index which lists most films on child development. The organisation is involved with linking the activities of all those whose concern is with children and much research is also carried out. Conferences for members are also held.

National Marriage Guidance Council Book Department
Little Church Street
Rugby
Warwicks   Tel: 0788 73241
Many useful booklets and pamphlets are published.
Local Marriage Guidance Councils will provide Counsellors trained to work with older pupils in secondary schools.

National Association for Maternal and Child Welfare
Tavistock House North
Tavistock Square
London, WCM 9JG   Tel: 01-387 9760
Produce a number of publications.
Run a Parentcraft Advisory service which supports courses for the examinations set by the Association which are geared to different levels of ability.

National Society for Mentally Handicapped Children
86 Newman Street
London W1P 4AR   Tel: 01-636 2861
Publish many books and pamphlets and have a shop at the above address which stocks books and toys.

National Council for One Parent Families
235 Kentish Town Road
London NW5 2LX   Tel: 01-207-1361
Formerly National Council for the Unmarried Mother and Her Child. Publications useful for teacher reading.

National Society for Prevention of Cruelty to Children
1 Riding House Street
W1P 8AA   01-580 8812
Information relating to preventative work of the society is interesting — particularly the Battered Baby units.
Will provide a speaker for schools but plenty of notice required.

The Spastics Society
12 Park Crescent, W1N 4EQ   01-636 5020
Produce leaflets and films on the work of the Society. Films must be
seen before showing to pupils.

Royal Society for the Prevention of Accidents
Royal Oak Centre
Brighton Road
Purley, Surrey. CR2 2UR   Tel: 01-688 4272
Produce leaflets, posters and booklets on all aspects of safety.

RESOURCES III

Suppliers of toys, etc

Creative Learning
Educational Supply Association
PO Box 22
Pinnacles
Harlow, Essex
A catalogue of all kinds of toys grouped into categories to fit various aspects of play. Also Paul and Marjorie Abbatt toys.

Galt Toys
30/31 Great Marlborough Street
W1   Tel: 01-734 0829
A toyshop with a variety of well designed toys. Catalogue available with toys graded to approximate ages

Goodwood Playthings
Lavant
Chichester, Sussex
Catalogue of good wooden toys

Play Specials
ESA
PO Box 22
Pinnacles, Harlow, Essex
Toys for handicapped children — carefully selected to give maximum learning experience.

RESOURCES IV

Carnation Foods Co Ltd
Medical Dept
Bush House
Aldwych WC2   Tel: 01-240 0891
Booklet *Your Contented Baby* about pregnancy, birth and physical care
of baby (free)

Cow & Gate (Unilever)
Mother & Baby Service
Guildford, Surrey   Tel: 0483 68181
Booklet — *From Cradle Days to Family Meals*

Gerber Baby Food
Division of CPD (UK) Ltd
Claygate House
Esher, Surrey
Booklet and menu cards on infant feeding

Glaxo-Farley Foods Division of Glaxo Laboratories Ltd
Torr Lane
Plymouth
Devon   Tel: 0752 701621
Leaflets on baby feeding and care

H J Heinz Co Ltd
Hayes Park
Hayes, Middx   Tel: 01-573 7757
From Milk to Mixed Diet — a guide to infant feeding

Sylvia Meredith
Health Education Advisory Service
3 Elgin Road
Sutton, Surrey
Provides posters, etc, from Mothercare

Mothercare Ltd
Cherry Tree Road
Watford, WD2 5SH   Tel: 92 25601
Shops in all main towns and shopping areas. Useful catalogues

National Dairy Council
National Dairy Centre
John Princes Street
London W1M OAP   Tel: 01-499 7822
Feeding the Under Fives — booklet suitable for class use

Smith & Nephew Ltd (makers of Elastoplast)
Welwyn Garden City, Herts   Tel: 96-25151
Free booklet on First Aid

Index

Compiled by Julian Hodgson

Adolescence 41-3, 78-9
Adoption 59-60
Aims and objectives of education
9
— of child care and development
courses 24, 25-35, 79-82
Au pair girls 15

Baby, growth and development
50-2
Books 40, 69-70
— adolescence 42
— conception and birth 49
— family and kinship 45
— growth and development of
baby 51
— growth and development of
young child 54, 57
— handicapped child 60
— language 74
— marriage 47
— play 73
See also chapter bibliographies
Broken homes 15

Child care and development
courses 13-14, 16, 81
— aims and objectives 24,
25-35, 79-82
— Adult Education Institutes
and 14
— best age for 13-14, 18-19
— effect of courses on pupils
20
— evaluation of 75-82
— for boys and/or girls? 14-15,
19-20
— Health Authorities and 14
— need for courses 8, 9-17, 77-8
— organisation and planning
18-24
    see also Curriculum
— outside teachers 22-4, 38

— pilot courses 7, 8, 18-19
— pupils' contribution 38
— teachers 21-2
— time spent on 20-21
— TV and 14
Child development
— baby 50-52
— young child 53-7
Child development courses
    See Child care and develop-
    ment courses
Child minders 63
Child rearing 10, 12, 50-57, 80
— central role of mother 10
— effects of degree of
urbanization 10
— — economic circumstances
10-11, 13
— — family size 10
— — poor housing 10-11, 13, 15
— — race 10, 80
— — sex 10
— — social class 10, 11-12, 15
— need for stability 30
See also Child care and development courses; Parenthood
Children in care 59-60
    See also Separations
Clinic *See* Family Health Centre
Communication 28, 30-33
    See also Language develop-
    ment; Play
Community education 19
Community service 20
Conception and birth 48-9
Cooking *See* Home economics
Curriculum
— design 27
— planning 18-24, 25-8
— suggestions for
— — adolescence 41-3
— — birth 22
— — children 5-13, 36

— — conception and birth 36, 48-9
— — Day Care 23
— — family and kinship 36, 44-5
— — family health 22
— — Family Health Centre 22, 61
— — family planning 22
— — first aid 23
— — food for the family 20
— — growth and development of a baby 50-52
— — growth and development of a young child 53-7
— — handicapped child 59-60, 61-2
— — home maintenance 20
— — home nursing 23
— — making clothes 20
— — making toys 20, 62, 63, 64
— — marriage 36, 44-5
— — maturity and old age 36
— — role play 64
— — Social Services Department 23
— — visits 20, 61-72
  See also individual places, eg Family Health Centre
— timetabling 20-21
— unit scheme 36-41
CSE See Examinations
Cycle of deprivation 11

Day Nurseries See Nursery groups
Discipline 12, 13, 14, 15, 78

Economic circumstances and child rearing 10-11, 13
Education, aims and objectives 9
— Of child care and development courses 24, 25-35, 79-82
Educational psychologist 23
Emotional growth 9

— lack of 11
— parental role 28-30
Emotional security 28, 29-30
Environment 12, 28
— effects on child rearing
— — of degree of urbanization 10
— — of economic circumstances 10-11, 13
— — of family size 10
— — of poor housing 10-11, 13, 15
— — of sex 10
— — of social class 10, 11-12, 15
— learning at home 10, 12
Environmental studies 19
Evaluation of courses 75-82
— multiple response tests 75, 76
— on tape 76
— continuous assessment 77
— practical work 76-7
— records of visits 76
— written work
  See also Examinations
Examinations 19, 76, 77
  See also Evaluation of courses

Family and kinship 9, 10, 28, 29, 44-5, 81-2
— disruption in 30
— need for stability 30
— separation from 29
— size 10
— — effect on language development 30-31
  See also Home
Family Health Centre 22, 61, 67
Father's role in child rearing 14, 20, 29
Film 40
— adolescence 42
— conception and birth 9
— family and kinship 45
— growth and development of a

baby 51-2
- growth and development of a young child 54, 57
- handicapped child 60
- language 74
- marriage 47
- play 73
Film strips and loops 40
- adolescence 42
- conception and birth 49
- growth and development of a baby 52
- growth and development of a young child 54-5
- play 73

Handicapped child 59-60, 61-2
Health Education Officer 22
Health Visitors 14, 22, 61, 63
Heredity 10, 12
Home, learning at 10, 12, 28
See also Environment
Home economics courses 9, 20, 63
Hospital 29, 61-2, 67
Housing
- and play 32-3
- poor 10-11, 13
- rehousing effects 15

Illiteracy *See* Reading ability; Language development
Inner London Education Authority, Home Economics Inspectorate 7
Inter-disciplinary studies 7, 19, 36
IQ levels 34

Language development 30-3, 74
Learning at home 10, 12, 28, 30-3
Low income families 10-11

Malnutrition 33-4

Marriage 9, 46-7
Maternity clinics 14, 32, 34
Mother
- age of conception 13
- as teacher on course 23
- central role in child rearing 10
- - child relationship 29-30
- - figure 29-30
Mothercare 62
Mothers' Clubs 33, 64, 67
Museums 62-3

National Child Development Study 80
Needlecraft courses 20
Nuffield Foundation 25
Nursery Groups 23, 33, 61, 64-72
See also Pre-school playgroups
Nutrition 28, 33-4, 63

Parent-child relationship 12, 29, 78
- affected by social class 10
Parental discipline 12, 13, 14, 15, 78
Parental role 28-30, 79, 81
Parenthood 13, 15
See also Child rearing; Teenage parents
Parenthood, preparation for, courses 7-8
- Adult Education Institutes and 14
- best age for 13-14
- Health Authorities and 14
- language development 32
- need for courses 9-17
- TV and 14

Physical care 33-4
Play 32-3, 70, 73
See also Toys
Playgroups *See* Pre-school Playgroups

Post-natal clinics 61
Pre-natal clinics *See* Maternity
    Clinics
Pre-school facilities 63
Pre-school playgroups 14, 20,
    23, 33, 61, 64, 65
— Playgroup advisers 23
    See also Nursery groups
Pre-school Playgroups Associat-
    ion 65
Problem families 11
Puppets 64

Racial differences 10
Radio *See* Television and radio
Reading ability 11
Resources 39-40
— adolescence 42-3
— conception and birth 49
— family and kinship 45
— growth and development of a
    baby 51-2
— growth and development of a
    young child 54, 57
— handicapped children 59-60
— marriage 47
    See also Resource list pp 85 ff

Save the Children Fund 65
Schools Council 25
— Enquiry on Young Leavers 78
— Project in Moral Education
    78-9
Scrap books 64
Separations 29
Sex differences 10
Single-parent families 15, 59-60
Social class
— age of conception related to
    13
— attitudes determined by 10,
    11-12, 15
— effects on child development
    12
Social Worker 23

Socialisation 10, 11, 15-16,
    29-30, 78
    See also Play
Stress 30

Tape recordings 40
— adolescence 43
— for evaluation of courses 76
— growth and development of a
    young child 55
— in playgroup situation 72
Tape/slide presentations 40
Teachers 21-4, 79
— in-service training 80-81
— need for preparation by 64,
    80-81
— outside workers as 24-4, 38
— — Day Nursery Matron 23, 66
— — Educational psychologist
    23
— — Health Education Officer
    22
— — Health Visitor 22
— — Parents 23
— — Playgroup advisors 23
— — Social Worker 23
Teaching packs 40
— adolescence 42
— conception and birth 49
— family and kinship 45
— growth and development of a
    young child 55, 57
— language 74
— marriage 47
— play 73
Technical studies 21
Teenage parents 13
Television and radio 40
Toilet training 11
Toy shops 62
Toys 20, 62, 63, 64

Urbanization, degree of
— effect on child rearing 10